MEXICO
in Pictures

Janice Hamilton

Lerner Books

London • New York • Minneapolis

Contents

INTRODUCTION — 4

THE LAND — 8

▶ Major Landforms. Rivers and Lakes. Climate. Flora and Fauna. States. Cities. Natural Resources. Environmental Problems.

HISTORY AND GOVERNMENT — 20

▶ Indigenous Peoples. The Maya. The Aztecs. Clash of Civilizations. The Spanish Colonial Period. Revolt in the Colony. An Independent Nation. The Porfiriato Dictatorship. Revolution. The Modern Era. Economic Strain. Democratic Reform. Rebellion in Chiapas. Moving into the Future. Government.

THE PEOPLE — 40

▶ A Diverse People. A Young, Urban Population. Health. Education.

Website address: www.lernerbooks.co.uk

First published in the UK in 2008 by Lerner Books, Dalton House, 60 Windsor Avenue, London SW19 2RR

web enhanced @ www.vgsbooks.com

CULTURAL LIFE 48

► Religion. Architecture and Art. Literature and Language. Media. Music and Dance. Holidays. Mexican Food. Sports.

THE ECONOMY 58

► Manufacturing, Oil and Mining. Service Industries. Agriculture. Infrastructure. Economic Challenges. Conclusion.

FOR MORE INFORMATION

► Timeline 66
► Fast Facts 68
► Currency 68
► Flag 69
► National Anthem 69
► Famous People 70
► Sights to See 72
► Glossary 74
► Selected Bibliography 75
► Further Reading and Websites 77
► Index 78

This edition was updated and edited for UK publication by Discovery Books Ltd., Unit 3, 37 Watling Street, Leintwardine, Shropshire SY7 0LW

British Library Cataloguing in Publication Data

Mexico. - (Visual geography series)
  1. Mexico - Juvenile literature
  972

ISBN-13: 978 1 58013 450 7

Printed in Singapore

INTRODUCTION

Mexico is a brilliant tapestry of colours, with whitewashed walls, blue skies, sienna deserts, lush green jungles, gold church altars and terracotta tiles. It is a patchwork of landscapes, from snow-peaked volcanoes to desert plateaus and sparkling beaches. And it is a vibrant blend of ancient cultures with modern cities and industries.

Mexico lies at the southern end of North America, sharing a border with the United States of America in the north and Belize and Guatemala in the south. Its western coast faces the Pacific Ocean, while the eastern shores overlook the Gulf of Mexico and the Caribbean Sea. In many ways, Mexico forms a bridge between North and South America. Biologically, for example, plant and animal species from both continents thrive in Mexico.

Culturally, Mexico shares a great deal with its Latin American neighbours. With 100 million people, it is the world's most populous Spanish-speaking country. Most Mexicans are of mixed European and native ancestry.

Economically, there are two Mexicos: the urban, industrialized, relatively prosperous north and the poor, rural south. The majority of the population lives in the northern cities. The largest cities include the capital, Mexico City, Guadalajara, Puebla and Monterrey.

Mexico has several distinct geographical regions, and it is rich in natural resources, including oil, silver, gold, iron and zinc. Mexico is the world's leading silver producer and fifth largest oil producer. Agriculture is also important to the economy, with crops including corn, wheat, sugar cane, coffee, fruit and vegetables.

Mexico's history can be divided into four main periods. Hunters and gatherers were the first inhabitants. Archaeologists have found the remains of a twenty-thousand-year-old campfire, along with stone and bone artefacts, near Puebla. By 1500 BC villages appeared, and starting in about AD 250, a series of advanced civilizations, including the Maya and the Aztecs, dominated the region. This first period ended in 1521, when Spanish conquistadors (conquerors) defeated the Aztecs.

The Spanish colonial period lasted for three hundred years, until a ten-year war culminated with Mexican independence in 1821.

During the next ninety years, the new nation tried out a variety of political models, from a short-lived empire to the thirty-year dictatorship of Porfirio Díaz. This period also included a war with the United States of America and an invasion by France. The final period, the modern era, began with the Mexican Revolution (1910–1920), a crucial event in the nation's history. The Constitution of 1917 shaped Mexico's future.

For seventy-one years, Mexican politics were dominated by one political party, the Institutional Revolutionary Party or PRI (for Partido Revolucionario Institucional, in Spanish). PRI officials and politicians were known for corruption and elections were even rigged to ensure PRI victories. In 2000 Mexico turned towards full democracy, with a fair election and a new president, Vicente Fox, who was not a member of the PRI.

In the late 1980s, Mexico embraced free trade, making agreements with a number of countries to encourage cross-border trade and investment. Despite some ups and downs, Mexico's economy grew rapidly. By the beginning of the twenty-first century, almost one-quarter of Mexicans were working in manufacturing and industry, making products such as beer, cigarettes, household appliances, cement, tyres, cars and lorries.

Mexico faces many problems, including the need to eliminate corruption among police and government officials and to control powerful drug smugglers. A crucial challenge is to help reduce poverty among the indigenous (native) peoples, especially in the south. Indigenous peoples have been fighting for their rights since 1994 in a rebellion in Chiapas, a state in southern Mexico. Other difficulties include chronic water shortages, environmental pollution, deforestation, soil erosion and the loss of skilled workers to the United States. Despite these challenges, Mexico remains a vibrant society and many Mexicans are optimistic about the future.

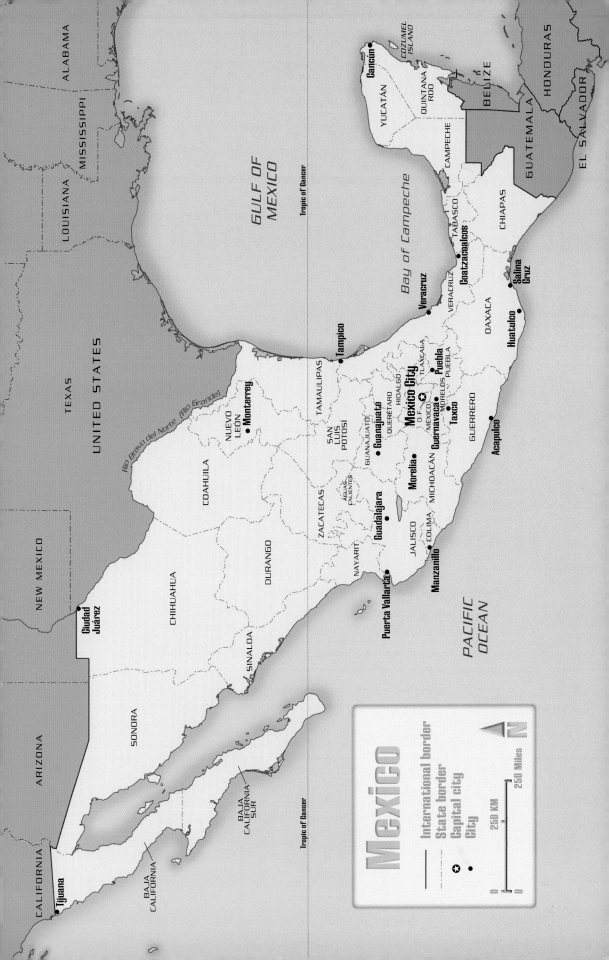

THE LAND

▷ Major Landforms

Mexico forms the southern part of North America. It shares its northern border with the US states of California, Arizona, New Mexico and Texas. Its southern border is shared with the Central American countries of Belize and Guatemala. The 9,330-kilometre (5,800-mile) coastline meets the Pacific Ocean to the west, while the Gulf of Mexico and the Caribbean Sea lap Mexico's eastern shores. Mexico is around eight times the size of the United Kingdom, covering a total area of 1,923,040 square kilometres (742,489 square miles). On a map, the country is shaped like a horn, with the Yucatán Peninsula forming the curved mouthpiece and the US border forming the broad rim.

This extremely diverse land ranges from vast deserts to tropical rainforests and from coastal lowlands to snowy peaks. The largest region is the Mexican Plateau, which rises gradually from about 915 metres above sea level at the US border to about 2,440 m at its southern end, just south of Mexico City.

The arid northern part of the plateau, the Mesa del Norte, is dotted with low mountains. The Chihuahuan Desert, extending across three Mexican states and into the United States, is the largest desert in North America. Further south is the Mesa Central, the heartland of Mexico. Between the mountains rising from this plateau are several basins, including the Valley of Mexico and the Guanajuato Basin. Spanning the southern end of the plateau is the Cordillera Neo-Volcánica. This impressive group of volcanoes includes Orizaba (also called Citlaltépetl), the country's highest point at 5,700 m, Ixtaccihuatl and Popocatépetl. The volcanic soil is very fertile and supports plentiful harvests.

The Mexican Plateau is hemmed in between two long mountain chains, the Sierra Madre Occidental in the west and the Sierra Madre Oriental in the east. Rivers flowing towards the Pacific Ocean have carved deep canyons in the Sierra Madre Occidental. The most spectacular is Barranca del Cobre, or Copper Canyon.

To the east of the Sierra Madre Oriental is the Gulf Coastal Plain. This swampy region is more than 160 km wide at its northern end but narrows in the south. The limestone that underlies the Gulf Coastal Plain also forms the base of the low, flat Yucatán Peninsula.

South-west of the Yucatán are more mountainous regions, including the Chiapas Highlands. The narrow, low-lying Isthmus of Tehuantepec connects this area to the rest of Mexico.

Along the Pacific Coast between the Gulf of Tehuantepec and Puerto Vallarta is another series of mountains, the Sierra Madre del Sur. These mountains are relatively low and the beautiful coastal area is a favourite with tourists. Further north, the Pacific Coastal Lowlands form a long strip of terraces, basins and river deltas between the Sierra Madre Occidental and the ocean.

Just south of the US state of California is a 1,290-km-long (800-mile-long) finger of arid land known as the Baja California Peninsula. Its granite peaks rise to more than 2,700 m. Between the Baja Peninsula and mainland Mexico lies the Gulf of California, also known as the Sea of Cortez.

Underlying Mexico's dramatic landscape is a geologically unstable junction of tectonic plates, the moveable segments that make up the earth's crust. When these plates move, the earth heaves and shakes.

Isla Espíritu Santo, an island off the eastern coast of the Baja California Peninsula, draws thousands of tourists every year.

Mexico has been the site of numerous earthquakes, including a 1985 earthquake that destroyed thousands of buildings in Mexico City. This plate junction also explains Mexico's volcanic activity, including eruptions of Popocatépetl in 1996 and 2000.

Rivers and Lakes

Most rivers in Mexico are no more than a few hundred kilometres long and are found in the south-east. Mexico's most famous river is Rio Bravo del Norte, also known as the Rio Grande. It begins in Colorado and flows almost 3,000 km (1,900 miles) to the Gulf of Mexico. It marks the border between the United States and Mexico for about 2,100 km (1,300 miles), rushing through wild canyons before meandering across the coastal plains. The river has been badly polluted by sewage, mining wastes and other toxins.

Vast regions of Mexico, including Baja California, have no surface water at all. In north-western Mexico, the Rivers Yaquí and Fuerte flow down from the Sierra Madre Occidental and cross the coastal plains to empty into the Gulf of California.

Rivers arising on the Mesa Central flow to both the east and west coasts. The major rivers in this region are the Pánuco, the Papaloapan and the Lerma. The Rio Balsas originates in the highlands of Puebla, south of the Mexican Plateau and flows into the Pacific. The Rio Grijalva and its main tributary, the Rio Usumacinta, drain the highlands of Guatemala and southern Mexico, flowing into the Bay of Campeche in the Gulf of Mexico. The Usumacinta forms part of Mexico's border with Guatemala.

Among Mexico's few lakes, Lake Chapala is the largest natural lake, measuring 80 km (50 miles) long and 16 km (10 miles) wide. It empties into the Rio Santiago, which cuts north-west through the Sierra Madre Occidental towards the Pacific.

Many wealthy Mexicans from nearby Guadalajara, as well as Americans and Canadians, have built homes along the shores of

IT ISN'T EASY LIVING NEXT DOOR TO AN ACTIVE VOLCANO

Popocatépetl has erupted several times in its twenty-five-thousand-year lifetime, but it put on its largest show in decades around Christmas 2000. The volcano sent molten rock high into the air, forcing forty-one-thousand residents of nearby villages to flee for several days. The volcano's name means 'smoking mountain' in the Nahuátl language, but most local people just call it El Popo and think of it as an old friend. Scientists keep a close watch on the volcano's activity so they can warn people of impending eruptions.

Motorized boats bob on the surface of Lake Chapala.

beautiful Lake Chapala. The shallow lake is polluted, however, and is slowly drying up.

Climate

Mexico's climate is as varied as its landscape. The hottest daytime temperatures reach 43°C in Baja California and the Sonoran and Chihuahuan Deserts in July and August, while regions at higher elevations are relatively cool.

South of the Mexican Plateau, elevation determines the local climate. From sea level to 900 m is known as the *tierra caliente,* or hot land. The *tierra templada,* or temperate land, extends from about 900 to 1,800 m. *Tierra fria,* the cold land, goes up to about 3,350 m. The *tierra helada,* or frozen land, with permanent snow, is at the highest elevations.

North of the Tropic of Cancer, which bisects the Mexican Plateau, there is little precipitation. In Chihuahua, for example, an average of just 0.2 centimetres of rain falls in April. Even July, the height of the wet season, brings only 8 cm of rain.

Areas near the Gulf of Mexico and Caribbean Sea are more humid. Veracruz, for example, gets 38 cm of rain in July, although 2.5 cm typically falls in January. Parts of the state of Tabasco get an average of 250 cm of rain each year, making it the country's wettest spot. The coastal lowlands are also hot, with average high temperatures from about 21° to 30°C throughout the year.

Summer is the wet season in the tropical regions of Mexico. Hurricanes, spawned in either the Pacific or Atlantic Oceans, sometimes hit the coasts between August and October.

◐ Flora and Fauna

Mexico ranks among the world's top five countries in biodiversity, or variety of plants and animals. This rich diversity occurs because Mexico has both North and South American species, and because it has many different ecosystems, ranging from deserts and coniferous forests to tropical rainforests and coral reefs.

About thirty thousand plant species grow in Mexico, including the boojum tree, a cactus resembling a bristly finger that can grow to 15 m tall. In the Yucatán Peninsula, the sapodilla, also known as the chicozapote tree, is the source of chicle, used as the basis of chewing gum.

In the dry scrublands and deserts of northern Mexico, grasses, shrubs, cacti and succulents such as agave are adapted to survive the harsh conditions. The Sonoran Desert is the most diverse desert in the world, with about three hundred species of cactus, including the prickly pear and the saguaro, which resembles a tall, thin man with his arms up in the air.

The vast plateau and mountain slopes of the Mesa Central are covered with oak and pine forests. Most of the Pacific coastal region is covered by deciduous or semi-deciduous forest. The tropical rain-forests in the rainy regions along the Gulf Coast, as well as in the Chiapas Highlands, support a diverse array of plants and trees, including hardwoods, palm trees and ferns. Mangrove thickets, marshes, lagoons and beaches flank the coastline.

Tall, gangly boojum trees thrive in Mexico's many deserts.

The majestic *ceiba* tree was considered sacred by the ancient Maya because it connected the Earth with the heavens. The flat-topped crowns of these tropical trees, which tower over the rain-forests, provide homes for countless birds, animals and plants.

Under the Caribbean waters off the Yucatán Peninsula lies the northern tip of the Mayan Coral Reef, one of the world's great barrier reefs. It is home to more than two hundred species of tropical fish.

The Gulf of California is one of the most diverse marine (sea) environments in the world because it has a rich supply of nutrients and receives so much sunlight. More than thirty species of marine mammals, including sea lions, dolphins and several types of whales, live here, as well as an abundance of bird and fish species.

Mexico has more than 450 species of mammals, including 140 that are found nowhere else. Land mammals include spider monkeys, howler monkeys, peccaries (relatives of the pig), desert bighorn sheep, jaguars, ocelots and mountain lions. The coastal waters are home to giant blue whales, grey whales, porpoises and manatees.

Parrots

The country is a bird-watcher's delight, with about one thousand species, including hummingbirds, parrots and flamingos. The quetzal, a tropical bird native to the Yucatán, was the sacred bird of the ancient Maya.

Mexico has the second largest number of reptile species in the world. They include geckos, crocodiles, iguanas, Gila monsters, desert tortoises, rattlesnakes and seven types of sea turtles.

◉ States

Mexico is divided into thirty-one states and a federal district around the capital. The most heavily populated areas are the state of México, the Distrito Federal and the central states of Jalisco, Guanajuato and Puebla. The states of Durango, Chihuahua and Zacatecas are in the north, while Chiapas and Oaxaca are the southernmost states.

Veracruz and Tabasco overlook the Gulf of Mexico, while Guerrero faces the Pacific. Baja California Sur has the smallest population. In physical size, Tlaxcala, north-east of the capital, is the smallest state and Chihuahua the largest.

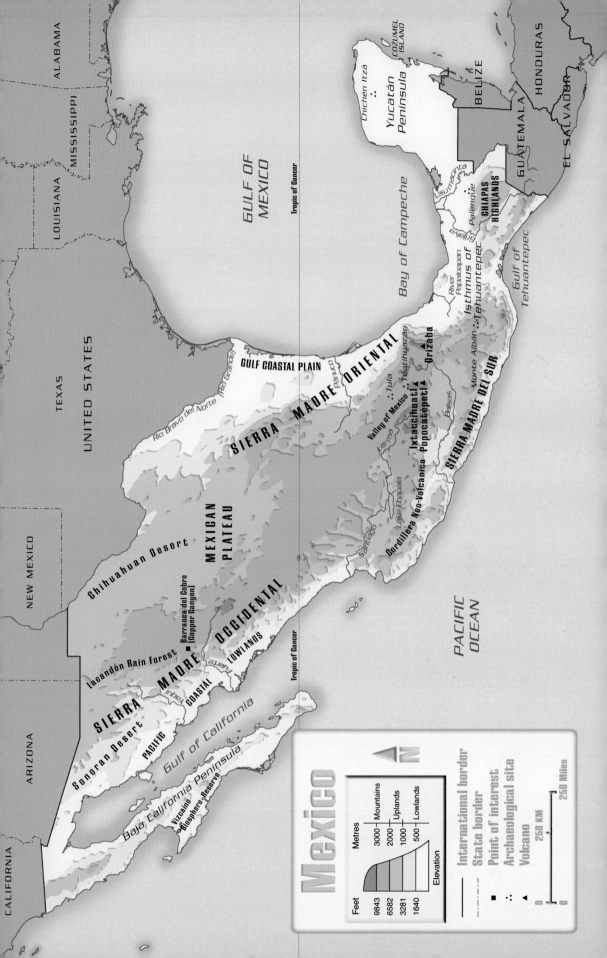

◉ Cities

MEXICO CITY Mexico City dates back to the 1300s, when the Aztecs built a settlement on an island in Lake Texcoco, which was later drained completely. According to legend, the Aztecs chose the spot after seeing an eagle perched on a cactus and eating a snake, a sight believed to fulfil an omen. This settlement became the Aztec capital, Tenochtitlán. Spanish explorer Hernán Cortés defeated the Aztecs in 1521, destroyed the buildings of Tenochtitlán, and immediately began construction of a new city, renamed Mexico, on top of the Aztec ruins.

The city was the seat of government for the Spanish colony and when Mexico gained independence, Mexico City became the capital. In the late 1800s and early 1900s, the city developed with new buildings and modern services, such as electric lights. Since then, millions of people from rural areas have flocked to Mexico City to seek work. Growth has slowed, partly as a result of job creation in other cities.

With more than eight million people, Mexico City is the tenth largest city in the world. The metropolis sprawls from its historic centre to cover an area of more than 7,300 sq km (4500 sq miles) and has a population of more than 20 million people, making it the third most populous metropolitan area in the world. Many wealthy and middle-

class residential areas lie to the south, while industries and impoverished shanty towns are in the northern sections.

Mexico City is rich in treasures, including ancient ruins, splendid murals, the biggest church in Latin America and the world's largest bullfighting ring. The bustling city never stops. Street vendors sell their wares to tourists visiting the shrine of the Virgin of Guadalupe. Families relax and play at Alameda Park. Mariachi bands and organ-grinders entertain pedestrians on street corners. Fans flock to the huge Azteca Stadium to watch football games.

Many industries are based in Mexico City, making products such as chemicals and plastics. Financial services and government offices are also concentrated in the city. There have never been enough jobs for everyone. Mexico City has vast slums known as *ciudades perdidas*, or 'lost cities'. The worst slums are built on rubbish dumps, where people survive by picking through rubbish, using or selling whatever they find.

The air in Mexico City has long ranked among the most badly polluted in the world. Pollution comes from industry and exhaust from cars and poorly maintained diesel lorries. The surrounding mountains block winds that could disperse the pollution and smog remains trapped in the valley. Thousands of people die each year of respiratory ailments. However, the government has had some success in improving air quality.

OTHER CITIES With a population of more than 1.6 million residents, Guadalajara is Mexico's second largest city. Founded in 1531, the historic city is renowned for its majestic cathedral, governor's palace, plazas and other Spanish colonial architectural gems. Most of the country's electronics, computer, telecommunications and software industries are based in Guadalajara.

A tree-lined boulevard in the centre of Mexico City, Paseo de la Reforma is one of the capital city's main streets. If you'd like to go on a virtual tour of Mexico City, go to vgsbooks.com to find links.

Mexico's third largest city, Puebla, also founded in 1531, is home to more than 1.5 million people. Many of its historic buildings and churches are decorated with the colourful pottery tiles unique to the area. Puebla is the capital of Puebla state and is an agricultural and industrial centre.

Monterrey, in the north-west, was built at the site of a natural spring more than four hundred years ago. Located on a railway to Laredo, Texas, it became a centre for heavy industry. This busy, modern, polluted city, with a population of more than one million, has ore processing plants and factories that make steel, cigarettes, plastics, foods and other products.

Acapulco, once the main Pacific port in Mexico, was developed in the 1940s as the country's first tourist resort. Located on a beautiful bay, the city attracted wealthy holidaymakers and celebrities. It must compete for sun-loving tourists with newer resorts such as Cancún, on the Yucatán Peninsula. Acapulco has a population of about 718,000.

Hot, humid Veracruz is a port city of approximately 425,000 people on the Gulf of Mexico. Mexico's gateway to the world for centuries, Veracruz remains an important port, out of which steel, cement, vehicles and other products are shipped, and into which sorghum (a grain), beans and vehicle parts are imported.

The twisted streets and narrow alleys of Guanajuato, in central Mexico, are built on barren hills that once provided huge quantities of silver and gold to be shipped to Spain. This small city boasts many historic mansions and churches.

Natural Resources

Mexico is rich in natural resources, including oil, minerals and forests. Large oil reserves lie under the Gulf of Mexico in Veracruz and Tabasco states. Mexico is the world's largest silver producer, and gold is found near Guanajuato and in Sonora and Durango states. Other resources that are mined include iron, copper, lead, zinc, sulphur and manganese.

When the Spaniards first landed in Mexico in the 1500s, forests covered two-thirds of the country. As a result of massive deforestation only about one-fifth of the land remains forested. Forest resources include valuable tropical hardwoods such as mahogany and rosewood, as well as pine and other softwoods from coniferous forests.

Fish were not considered a significant commercial resource until the mid-1900s. Fleets of fishing boats troll the Gulfs of Mexico and California for seafood. Sardines, anchovies and tuna are fished off Baja California. Mexico's pleasant climate, spectacular beaches, varied scenery, historic buildings and archaeological treasures are all resources that attract tourists and generate jobs for Mexicans.

Environmental Problems

Despite its natural beauty, Mexico faces a number of serious environmental problems. Deforestation has occurred at one of the fastest rates in the world. However commercial logging is not the biggest culprit. Large rainforests have also been cleared for cattle ranching. Unique plants and animals are disappearing along with the trees.

Overgrazing by livestock and soil erosion also pose threats. As soil is worn away or destroyed, agricultural land becomes unproductive. The worst erosion is happening in northern states such as Sonora.

Water shortages present another environmental challenge. Mexico is chronically short of water for industry and irrigation, since the heavily populated and agricultural areas are in the dry north, while the wetter south is far from the centre of activity. Many manufacturing plants have been built near the US border, and farmers in the area complain that the water they need to irrigate their crops is going to these factories instead.

Critics say that environmental issues have not been dealt with effectively in Mexico. They accuse the government of contributing to pollution by not regulating companies that pollute. However, many Mexican citizens are too busy struggling to earn a living to demand improvements in environmental policy, and they have not had a strong tradition of protecting wildlife and nature. The government has made some conservation efforts, however. For example, several national parks and protected areas called biosphere reserves have been set aside.

BUTTERFLY WINTER HOME IS THREATENED

Every autumn, millions of black-and-orange monarch butterflies from eastern and central Canada and the United States converge on a small, mountainous region west of Mexico City, near the city of Morelia. They spend the winter resting on the limbs of oyamel fir trees, then mate and head north again in the spring.

Although the area was set up as a butterfly sanctuary in 1986, illegal tree logging has continued. Some fear that the loss of trees threatens the butterflies' survival.

In 2000 the Mexican government and several international conservation organizations announced a project to expand the butterfly reserve, pay the people of the area to stop logging, and train them for jobs in tourism.

HISTORY AND GOVERNMENT

▶ Indigenous Peoples

Evidence of Mexico's earliest inhabitants lives on in stone and bone artefacts and in the remains of a twenty-thousand-year-old campfire near Puebla. The people who sat around that campfire were hunters who used slings and spears to kill mammoths, camels, bison and smaller animals. They also collected mesquite beans, prickly pear cactus fruit and piñon nuts to eat.

In about 7000 BC, central and northern Mexico became hotter and drier, and the big game disappeared. People hunted small animals, caught fish in nets, made baskets and wove cotton and other fibres. Agriculture started in Mexico about this time, as people began to plant beans, squash and maize, or corn. Maize, ground and made into porridge or tortillas, became a central part of the diet.

By 2000 BC, indigenous Mexicans lived in permanent villages. They supplemented their basic diet of corn, beans and squash with foods from native plants, such as chilli peppers, avocados and vanilla.

They smoked tobacco leaves and made beer from agave plants.

The earliest known civilization in Mexico was that of the Olmecs, which flourished from about 1200 to 400 BC. Archaeologists have found Olmec sites, including huge stone sculptured heads, near Veracruz.

The Maya

One of the most sophisticated ancient civilizations in all of the Americas was established by the Maya. The Maya achieved prominence in Mexico's central lowlands, the Chiapas Highlands, the Yucatán Peninsula and Central America. The first and greatest period of Maya culture lasted from about AD 300 to 900. The people built large centres such as Palenque, with magnificent limestone pyramids and palaces with arched openings. Brightly coloured frescoes on the walls of important buildings showed dancers, musicians, warrior, and slaves. The Maya made beautiful pottery, as well as gold ornaments, jade jewellery and copper tools.

The Maya had extensive knowledge of astronomy, which was linked to their beliefs about the way the gods controlled destiny and the way time repeated itself in cycles. They worked out an accurate solar calendar and could predict solar and lunar eclipses. They also developed a number system with three symbols (a dot for one, a bar for five and a shell-like figure for zero). The people recorded their history using about eight hundred different hieroglyphs – picture symbols – that have only recently been decoded.

The Maya lived in independent city-states that fought and traded with each other. The hereditary nobility, including priests and high officials and their families, formed the upper class. Most of the common people were farmers, but there were also skilled craftspeople and slaves. No one knows exactly what happened to the Maya, but around AD 950 the great centres were abandoned. Later, a revived Maya civilization fused with the Toltec people in the Yucatán Peninsula. The Toltecs introduced large-scale human sacrifice. One of their many gods was Quetzalcóatl, the feathered serpent.

The Maya played a ball game called *pok-a-tok*, which probably originated with the Olmecs around 500 BC. It was played in a walled-in field about the size of two tennis courts. Points were scored by passing the ball through small stone rings. The game had religious significance, and the heavy rubber ball may have symbolized the sun, while the rings represented the spring and fall equinoxes. Members of the losing team were often put to death.

Other indigenous groups that also developed advanced cultures were the Zapotec and Mixtec Indians in the Oaxaca region. The main Zapotec city from about AD 200 to 900 was at Monte Albán. The Mixtecs dominated the region from Oaxaca to southern Puebla from the 600s to the arrival of the Spaniards hundreds of years later. Mixtec artisans made jewellery from pearl, turquoise, jet, gold, and silver, and they wrote their history in codices, or books made of deerskin.

Meanwhile, other indigenous groups controlled the Mexican Plateau. The city of Teotihuacán, north-east of present-day Mexico City, was probably built between AD 100 and 200. At its peak population of 125,000 (around AD 400 to 500), Teotihuacán was the largest city in the Americas. The people irrigated their crops and used sophisticated engineering techniques. They carved elaborate stone pyramids and made weapons, tools and ornaments from obsidian, a volcanic glass. Through military dominance, trade and religious influence, they

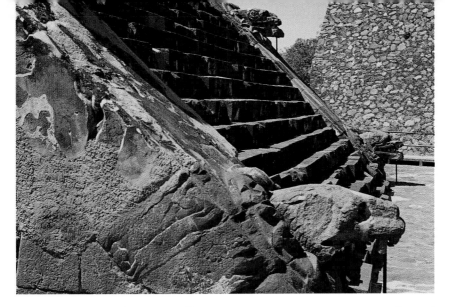

The magnificent ruins of Teotihuacán encompass many stone tombs and pyramids. To see more pictures of ruins in Mexico, go to vgsbooks.com for links.

had a great impact across a broad region. The reason for the civilization's decline in the 700s is still not known.

After the fall of Teotihuacán, the Toltec empire continued to flourish from about 900 to 1200. The main city was at Tula, not far from Teotihuacán. Legends of Toltec achievements, mixed with religious myth, have survived into modern times. In the 1100s, enemies invaded Tula and burned the ceremonial buildings. The city's leaders fought among themselves, and most of the residents left. Between 1200 and 1500, no dominant civilization thrived on the plateau.

The Aztecs

The Aztecs created Mexico's last great indigenous civilization. They descended from two groups of ancestors: the Toltecs and a semi-nomadic people, the Mexica, who had invaded the Valley of Mexico from the north.

The Aztecs built the city of Tenochtitlán on an island in Lake Texcoco, one of five lakes in the area. This location was easy to defend and permitted the residents to trade by canoe with other villages and city-states in the valley.

The Aztecs were good engineers. They solved the problem of lack of farmable land by putting mud on rafts anchored to the lake bottom and growing crops on these floating gardens. They enlarged the island and built canals to control flooding, waterways through the marshes for canoe travel, causeways (raised roads) to the mainland and an aqueduct to bring fresh spring water to the city.

The elite of Aztec society included nobility, warriors and priests, who acted as government advisors and oversaw ceremonies involving human sacrifice. The Aztecs believed that human blood was food for the gods. Human sacrifice was also helpful in terrorizing and eliminating enemies.

The Aztecs formed an alliance with leaders of two other large city-states and came to dominate an empire that, by 1515, included most of central and southern Mexico. The empire grew rich as traders carried obsidian weapons, cloth and rope south and brought back shells, cacao beans, rubber and gold.

Clash of Civilizations

After Christopher Columbus's voyage to the Americas in 1492, Spanish colonists began to explore and occupy parts of the Caribbean. In 1519 Spanish soldier Hernán Cortés led an expedition that included about five hundred experienced soldiers and sixteen horses. They set sail from Cuba, a Spanish colony and landed near present-day Veracruz, Mexico.

From his palace in Tenochtitlán, the Aztec emperor Moctezuma II heard about the arrival of the Cortés expedition. Moctezuma was unsure how to treat the newcomers. He did not know whether they were enemies or gods. He sent messengers with gifts of gold to try to discourage Cortés from coming to the city. The gold just made Cortés

more determined to reach the centre of the Aztec empire. Before marching to Tenochtitlán, Cortés had to repress a threatened mutiny of his own soldiers. He sank all his ships so his men could not retreat to Cuba. Then he formed alliances with other Indian groups, including the Tlaxcalans, who resented the harsh way the Aztecs had treated them.

On 8 November, 1519, Cortés's expedition reached Tenochtitlán, and Moctezuma and Cortés met face to face. At first, they treated each other with great respect and exchanged

After a long and trying journey, Spanish explorer Cortés met Moctezuma in the Aztec capital city of Tenochtitlán.

jewellery and other gifts. Doña Marina, Cortés's native mistress, acted as one of the interpreters. Within a week of the Spaniards' arrival, however, they had Moctezuma under arrest in his own palace.

For a time, Moctezuma helped Cortés, but the relationship soured after a hotheaded Spanish officer massacred a large crowd of Aztecs who were gathered for a celebration. In June 1520, some Aztecs attacked the palace and cut off food supplies to the Spaniards. Moctezuma went to the palace rooftop and called on the Aztecs to stop the attack. According to Spanish accounts of the incident, someone threw a stone and hit Moctezuma on the head, killing him. The Aztecs said it was the Spaniards who killed the Aztec leader.

However it happened, Cortés decided the wise course was to retreat. He planned an escape to the mainland via a causeway for the night of 30 June. But he and his men were discovered, and more than half the Spaniards and one thousand of their native allies were killed in what has become known as *la noche triste* (the sad night).

Cortés regrouped and was joined by reinforcements of Spanish soldiers and Tlaxcalans. Over the following months, he conquered or allied himself with all the towns around Tenochtitlán. Then he laid siege to the capital. The Aztecs, under the leadership of Moctezuma's eighteen-year-old nephew, Cuauhtémoc, resisted for almost four months.

The Spaniards had many advantages: swords, cannons, horses and thirteen armed ships they built and launched on Lake Texcoco. The Aztecs had less powerful weapons and a city under siege. They also fell victim to a devastating smallpox epidemic that had been brought to Mexico by the Spaniards. The indigenous peoples had never been exposed to the deadly disease before, so they lacked immunity – their bodies could not fight off the smallpox virus.

Finally, on 13 August, 1521, with thousands of his people killed in battle or from starvation or disease and the city's palaces and pyramids destroyed by Cortés's troops, Cuauhtémoc was captured as he tried to escape. He was the last ruler – the Aztec empire was finished. Mexicans still revere Cuauhtémoc for his courageous resistance, while their feelings about Cortés the conqueror are less than warm.

◐ The Spanish Colonial Period

The Spaniards built a new city they called Mexico on top of the Aztec ruins at Tenochtitlán. They quickly gained control of southern Mexico, the Pacific coast, and the north-central silver-producing region. Mexico became part of New Spain, a colony that eventually stretched from the Caribbean to the Philippines and from Central America to California. Laws and regulations were passed in Spain, and in Mexico the Spanish government was represented by the viceroy, the top official in the colony.

Farming and ranching formed the base of colonial life. Agricultural production increased dramatically with the introduction from Europe of the plough, wheeled carts, metal tools, mules and other work animals. Most Spaniards lived in the cities, but some owned large rural properties called haciendas. They hired managers to run the haciendas, and day labourers worked for wages, living in shacks on the estates.

The Spanish government controlled all trade in New Spain. Silver, gold, tobacco, cacao, sugar, cotton and dyes were sent to Spain. The colonists imported clothing, books, furniture, olive oil and medicine. They were charged very high prices for these goods, and trade was made even more difficult by shipping delays, high taxes and many forms to fill out. But by the end of the eighteenth century, merchants were allowed to sail with few restrictions between Spain and colonial ports. As a result, business boomed, consumers paid lower prices, and fewer goods were smuggled.

The Spaniards were zealously religious, and converting the native peoples to Christianity was a top priority for the colonists. The first Roman Catholic missionaries arrived in Mexico in 1523, and they were soon followed by many other priests and nuns. Churches and cathedrals were constructed, often near indigenous sacred sites.

The Catholic Church played an important role in the colony. It ran schools and hospitals, cared for orphans and the poor, recorded births, deaths and marriages, and even provided business loans. It also amassed a great deal of wealth by collecting special church taxes called tithes, as well as land donated by pious individuals.

By 1534 there were several schools in Mexico City, but education was reserved for the Spanish elite and a few lucky native children. Girls rarely received an education.

The indigenous peoples of Mexico did not fare well in the colony of New Spain. While some Spaniards were supposed to protect native villages and convert the people to Christianity, the communities were obliged to pay tributes, or taxes, in return. When, as often happened, people could not pay in cash, they had to provide labour instead. Many indigenous farmers were forced to sell their crops at prices below fair value. Others lost their land when the newcomers seized it for their own crops and livestock.

Imported diseases wiped out millions of indigenous people. The native population declined from about 20 million before the Spanish arrived to about 3.3 million by 1570. It dipped to 1.3 million by 1646 before beginning to recover. However, the indigenous people were always the majority of the population in colonial Mexico.

Peninsulares, as European-born people were known, held all the high ranking positions in the government, army and church. They were at the top of the social ladder, above all those who were born in the colony.

People of European descent who were born in Mexico and rich Mexicans, including racially mixed children of wealthy Europeans, were known as Creoles. Many Creoles became lawyers, doctors or teachers, or they owned haciendas, mines and textile factories. Mestizos – people of mixed European and native background – formed much of the lower middle class, working as artisans, farmers and cowboys and in mines and missions. Many Africans also lived in the colony, imported to New Spain to work as slaves.

Mexico in the seventeenth century was a quiet place, enjoying political stability and some independence from Spain. The eighteenth century was much more turbulent. Because of threats to the colony's distant borders from the French, English, Russians and hostile native peoples, the Spanish government decided to build forts in the north and create a permanent army and militia in New Spain for the first time.

Taxes were oppressively high, both to pay the costs of protecting the colony and to keep the royal treasury full. Many Creoles resented their second-class status. Some people in the colony started to talk about self-government. The American Revolution in 1776 and the French Revolution in 1789 provided inspiration.

AFRICAN INFLUENCE

During the colonial period, some 200,000 black slaves were brought to Mexico. The colonists needed more workers because so many Indians had died during epidemics. Most of the slaves were men. Many had mixed-race children with Indian or white women. By 1810, there were 625,000 people of mixed black ancestry in the colony. By then most of the slaves had been freed. African rhythms and instruments, especially drums and marimbas, influenced Mexican music. The slaves' legends and tales became part of Mexican culture, and they brought other skills, such as carving, basket making and folk medicine.

Revolt in the Colony

On 16 September, 1810, Miguel Hidalgo y Costilla, a parish priest from Dolores, a small town about 55 km (35 miles) northeast of Guanajuato, rang the church bells, calling his parishioners together. He gave a speech demanding the expulsion of the peninsulares. He and his followers – townspeople, local miners, Indians, mestizos and prisoners

This mural by José Clemente Orozco, in a government building in Guadalajara, depicts the fury of Miguel Hidalgo y Costilla, (Father Hidalgo), a parish priest who became a revolutionary leader in 1810.

released from local jails – marched to Guanajuato. There, Hidalgo lost control of the large crowd of rebels, and several hundred elite Creoles were massacred. In March 1811, Hidalgo was captured and executed.

The next major revolt was led by another priest, José María Morelos y Pavón, who led small bands of mestizo and native fighters to take control of much of southern Mexico. In 1813 Morelos set up a congress that issued the first declaration of independence. A year later, he wrote a constitution that declared Mexico a republic, abolished slavery and eliminated all class distinctions. This constitution was never put into effect, but it did serve as a model for later documents. In 1815 Father Morelos was captured by government forces and killed.

Political unrest abated for several years until a new independence movement swept the country. Supporters of the movement held that Mexico was independent and Roman Catholic and that its people were united. The Creole-supported military hero Augustín de Iturbide joined forces with rebel leader Vicente Guerrero to fight for independence from Spain. The Treaty of Córdoba, signed by Iturbide and the last Spanish viceroy on 24 August, 1821, established Mexico as an independent country.

⊙ An Independent Nation

In 1822 Iturbide became Emperor Augustín I, but the empire lasted less than a year. A group of army officers forced the autocratic leader to give up his throne, and in 1824 he was executed. Mexico was proclaimed a federal republic, based on the American model, with a president, vice president, senate, chamber of deputies and nineteen states. However, the new republic lacked both experienced leaders and funds. In the republic's first fifty years, political power swung back and forth between liberal and conservative groups, and there were thirty different presidents.

The dominant figure of the early republic was General Antonio López de Santa Anna. He became a politician and served as president eleven times between 1833 and 1855. Clever and charismatic, he eventually became a dictator.

In the 1830s, trouble brewed in Texas, which was the northern part of Mexico at the time. Thousands of new colonists had started cotton farms there. They were mostly English-speaking Protestants and did not mix well with the Catholic, Spanish-speaking Mexicans.

When Texas declared independence from Mexico in 1836, General Santa Anna led a force to put down the revolt. The Mexicans defeated the Texans at an abandoned mission in San Antonio called the Alamo. The massacre rallied Texans to pursue their cause. Six weeks later, they defeated the Mexican army, and Santa Anna signed a peace treaty with the president of the Republic of Texas.

After a bloody defeat at the Alamo, Texan rebels became determined to separate from the rest of Mexico.

General Santa Anna

Still, Mexico did not recognize Texas as independent. When the US government annexed Texas in 1845, Mexico broke off diplomatic relations with the United States. War broke out between the United States and Mexico in 1846.

In 1847 the US government decided that the only way to win the war was to invade Mexico. US troops landed at Veracruz and occupied Mexico City. The war ended with the signing of the Treaty of Guadalupe Hidalgo in 1848. Under the treaty, Mexico lost two-fifths of its territory, including Texas and the land that became California, Nevada, Utah and parts of four other U.S. states. In 1853 the border moved again when Mexico sold New Mexico and part of Arizona to the United States for $10 million. Santa Anna needed the money to pay for his army and the lavish lifestyle he saw as befitting his new title, His Most Serene Highness.

In 1855 Santa Anna was removed from office, this time for good, in a liberal uprising. One of the rebel leaders was Benito Juárez, a well-educated Zapotec Indian. He and his colleagues in a movement called *La Reforma* (The Reform) wrote new laws based on ideals of social justice. Their goal was to reduce the power and special legal rights held by the Church and the military.

The Catholic Church owned almost half the land in Mexico, so the reformers passed a law preventing institutions from owning land. This forced the Church to sell property that was not used for religious purposes. The law's other result was that the *ejidos*, communal farms owned by Indian villages, were also destroyed. Consequently, many native people had to go to work as labourers for large landowners, who exploited them and did not provide social services, as the Church had.

The liberal reformers wrote a new constitution in 1857. It established Mexico as a democratic nation, set up a legislature, and defined the role of the states. The Constitution of 1857 abolished slavery, compulsory military service and all titles of nobility and it included a bill of rights that guaranteed freedom of speech. This important document remained unchanged until 1917.

Church leaders did not like the constitution, because many of their rights and duties had been stripped away. For example, the state, rather than the Church, was responsible for registering births, deaths and marriages. Military officers and aristocrats also resented the loss of their privileges. In 1858 a new revolt broke out. For a time, there were two governments. Juárez ran the liberal government from Veracruz, while the conservatives set up a rival government in Mexico City. The civil war ended with a liberal military victory, and in 1861 Juárez returned to Mexico City and was elected president. After this bitter conflict, unemployment was high and the country was bankrupt.

Meanwhile, France, Spain and Great Britain sent ships to Veracruz in 1862 to punish Mexico for not paying back its foreign loans. The French ruler Napoléon III also wanted to expand France's influence into Latin America. Spain and Great Britain withdrew their troops, but the French pressed on. The Mexicans held off the French invaders near Puebla on 5 May, 1862. France sent reinforcements, who invaded Mexico City in June 1863. One year later, the French installed an Austrian archduke, Ferdinand Maximilian, as emperor of Mexico.

Rather than bringing peace and orderly government to Mexico as he intended, Maximilian managed to annoy the army, the conservatives, the Church and the republicans. Napoléon III realized that his Mexican adventure had been a disaster and withdrew his troops. The republicans besieged Maximilian and his small army, and in June 1867, he and his generals were executed.

The Porfiriato Dictatorship

In 1867 Juárez was once again elected president, and his government set about revitalizing the economy. The government modernized the mining industry, encouraged export crops such as tobacco, cacao, sugar, cotton, coffee and vanilla, and promoted foreign investment. The Juárez administration also set up a new system of public education, since the Church no longer ran schools. Juárez died suddenly in 1872 and was succeeded by another reformer.

In 1876 Porfirio Díaz, a popular former military hero, seized power in a coup d'état (the sudden overthrow of an existing government). Díaz controlled the country as a dictator for more than thirty years, a period known as the Porfiriato. The army supported Díaz, as did the Catholic Church, which was again allowed to acquire property.

During the Porfiriato, Mexican cities and industries expanded and were modernized, funded by a combination of Mexican capital, U.S. and European investments and government subsidies. Electric streetlights and telephone systems were installed in several cities, and an extensive railway network was constructed. Steel, textile, chemical, paper and other manufacturing plants opened, and petroleum was also discovered.

The vast majority of Mexicans lived in rural areas and did not benefit from the economic and industrial progress in the cities. Almost

Although he ruled the country as a dictator for more than thirty years, Porfirio Díaz brought many important gains to Mexico. Under his regime, cities expanded, technological advances were made and modes of transport were improved.

all the farmable land belonged to the owners of a few enormous haciendas. Wages and living standards for almost all Mexicans were low, and working conditions in many factories were terrible. Illiteracy was high – 80 per cent of the population could not read.

In 1910 a popular landowner, Francisco Madero, challenged Díaz for the presidency, promising full democracy. Díaz threw Madero in jail and declared himself reelected. This was the last straw for many citizens. For the next ten years, Mexico was embroiled in a revolution.

Revolution

Most historians view the Mexican Revolution as the central event in the country's history. It brought together northern and southern Mexicans. It gave workers, peasants, middle-class professionals and radical intellectuals a sense of common purpose, as almost everyone joined in rebellion against the privileged few. The goals set out by the revolution became guidelines for future government policies. The goals included democratic elections and greater civil liberties, land redistribution, limits on foreign ownership of land, improved working conditions and controls on the wealth and political influence of the Catholic Church.

Rebel leaders Francisco 'Pancho' Villa and Emiliano Zapata are still celebrated as heroes of the revolution. But they were just two among thousands of people who struggled to bring about freedom. Fighting broke out in almost every major city in Mexico, and many villages and haciendas were completely destroyed. More than one million Mexicans died.

In 1914 the revolutionaries defeated the government forces, but they disagreed over who should control the country, and the revolution continued until 1920. At the end of the conflict, Mexico's rulers included business leaders, revolutionary generals and landowners who wanted to form a strong central government and modernize Mexico.

The main legacy of the revolution was the Constitution of 1917, which remains in force in modern Mexico. It includes the major features of the 1857 constitution, outlining the organization of the states, civil liberties and democratic principles. The 1917 constitution also gave the national government an active role in promoting the social, economic and cultural well-being of its citizens.

The constitution curtailed the Church's power by confiscating Church property and prohibiting the clergy from voting or discussing politics in public. It also called for redistribution of land to the peasants.

After the revolution, Plutarco Elías Calles dominated Mexican politics for ten years, first as president, then behind the scenes. In 1929 he organized the political party that eventually became known as the Partido Revolucionario Institucional (PRI), or Institutional Revolutionary Party.

Plutarco Elías Calles *(centre)*, pictured here with William Taft *(left)* and US president Calvin Coolidge *(right)*, founded the Partido Revolucionario Institucional (PRI) in 1929. This party dominated Mexican politics for decades.

Calles balanced the budget and oversaw improvements in social conditions and the construction of motorways, dams and irrigation projects. Between 1929 and 1934, however, Mexico was hit by the Great Depression, a worldwide period of economic decline. Unemployment soared and foreign trade fell.

The Modern Era

Beginning in the late 1930s, the Mexican government shifted its emphasis from agriculture and social programmes to becoming a more industrial, urban nation with a role on the world stage. In 1938 the government nationalized – took over ownership of – the petroleum industry, giving a monopoly to a new company called Petróleos Mexicanos, or PEMEX. Many Mexicans supported this step.

A mainstay of the Mexican economy since the turn of the twentieth century, the petroleum industry came under government control in 1938.

During World War II (1939–1945), Mexico supplied oil, copper, zinc and other raw materials to the Allies (Great Britain, the USA and allied nations). The war caused shortages of imported goods, so Mexican workers also began to produce glass, cement and other goods for the domestic market. After several Mexican oil tankers were torpedoed in 1942, the country declared war on the Axis powers (Germany, Italy and Japan), and a small group of Mexican airmen fought in the Pacific theatre.

In the 1950s, port facilities were constructed, irrigation and flood control measures were expanded and coastal lowlands were drained to eliminate breeding grounds for malaria-carrying mosquitoes. With better health care, life expectancy increased, and the population doubled between 1934 and 1958.

In 1968 Mexico City hosted the summer Olympic Games, but violence threw a shadow over the sporting events. During the months leading up to the games, university students held a series of demonstrations to protest the excessive amount of money being spent by the government on the Olympics. Shortly before the Olympic opening ceremonies, police fired on demonstrators at Tlatelolco Plaza on the outskirts of Mexico City. The government admitted that thirty-two people had died, but the number was more likely between two and three hundred. Two thousand protesters were arrested.

Economic Strain

After enjoying thirty years of post-war growth, a period that was dubbed the Mexican Miracle, the country ran into a series of economic crises starting in the mid-1970s. Its debt to foreign governments soared, and inflation increased by 20 to 30 per cent a year. In 1976 the government devalued the peso (Mexico's national currency). Instead of the 12.5 pesos previously needed to buy one U.S. dollar, more than 20 pesos were needed.

Then large reserves of petroleum were discovered in south-eastern Mexico. By 1980 Mexico had become the world's fifth largest oil producer. Many people thought the country's financial problems were over, but the oil industry created few jobs. Meanwhile, the government continued to borrow from foreign banks to pay for new roads, schools and other facilities. When world oil prices fell, Mexico could not repay its loans. The resulting economic crisis began in 1982 and lasted for several years. Unemployment soared, and the government had to cut spending. Many people were living in poverty.

Mexico's economy was still dominated by the government, which owned or controlled most basic industries, including steel, petroleum, communications, electrical utilities and banks. High taxes on imported goods were designed to protect Mexican-made products. The economic profile changed under the administration of President Carlos Salinas de Gortari, who came to power in 1988.

Salinas sold hundreds of poorly managed, state-owned companies to private investors. More important, Mexico joined the North American Free Trade Agreement (NAFTA) with the United States and Canada. Since NAFTA came into force in 1994, trade barriers, such as customs duties (taxes), have been removed gradually.

Mexico's entry into NAFTA also increased pressure on the government

Carlos Salinas de Gortari

to hold fair elections. With closer economic ties to the United States, Mexico became more sensitive to criticism of its poor record in preserving democratic processes.

Democratic Reform

Under the PRI, Mexico looked like a stable democracy. Every six years, an election took place, and since a president could serve only one term, power appeared to change hands peacefully. However, influenced by the PRI, presidents handpicked their successors, so the democratic process was only superficial. In addition, the PRI was not above electoral fraud. Crime and corruption were also widespread through police and government ranks.

The government also tried to silence its critics. The Mexican intelligence service taped the phone calls of opposition politicians and harassed, kidnapped or beat critics. Hundreds of anti-government activists are said to have disappeared during the last three decades of the twentieth century.

Although corruption remained rampant during the Salinas administration, electoral laws were reformed in 1990. The press became freer to criticize the government, and opposition voices became stronger. Salinas also amended the constitution to allow Catholic priests to vote, private schools to teach religion, and the Church to own property.

In 1994 the PRI's presidential candidate and another leading party official were assassinated. As a result of the murders, international observers were permitted to oversee the Mexican presidential election for the first time that year, and they determined that it was generally honest. The winner, Ernesto Zedillo Ponce de León, was a US-trained economist.

Less than one month after Zedillo took office, economic disaster struck again when the peso suddenly dropped to half its former value.

To help Mexico avoid total economic collapse, the US government and international agencies loaned the government billions of dollars.

Zedillo blamed the financial crisis on Salinas. Salinas's brother Raúl was found guilty of ordering one of the 1994 assassinations. Another powerful PRI official was found guilty of taking bribes from drug traffickers, and Carlos Salinas left the country in disgrace.

Rebellion in Chiapas

When Mexico joined the North American Free Trade Agreement, agriculture laws were changed and Mexican farmers lost all hope of ever receiving good land. On 1 January, 1994, the date when NAFTA took effect, a group of farmers and Indians in the southern state of Chiapas launched an armed revolt against the government. The conflict centred around indigenous rights, land redistribution and economic development.

Led by a mysterious, pipe-smoking man in a ski mask named Subcommander Marcos (who is a former university professor), the rebels called themselves the Zapatista National Liberation Army, or Zapatistas, after the revolutionary hero Emiliano Zapata. Among the Zapatistas' demands were land, schools, roads, hospitals and tractors.

As head of the Zapatista National Liberation Army, Subcommander Marcos launched a revolt against the Mexican government in 1994.

The first phase of the rebellion lasted ten days, resulting in about 140 deaths. The government sent in the army, and thousands of Indians in the area fled for safety. The conflict reheated in 1997, when civilians who supported the government armed and organized themselves like an army unit and massacred forty-five people, mainly women and children, in the village of Acteal.

Visit vgsbooks.com for links to websites where you can find out more about the Mexican Revolution, the people of Chiapas and the Zapatistas, the current Mexican government and President Vicente Fox.

◑ Moving into the Future

By 2000 the PRI's long run was coming to an end. About one-third of state governors were members of opposition parties, and more than half the population lived in cities run by non-PRI mayors. In the 2000 presidential election, two main political parties, the Democratic Revolution Party and the National Action Party (PAN, for Partido de Acción Nacional) opposed the PRI. The PAN candidate, Vicente Fox, emphasized change. He promised to resolve the ongoing rebellion in Chiapas, fight government corruption, improve education and reduce poverty. He won by a small margin, but with the support of young, urban, middle-class Mexicans.

Immediately after taking power, President Fox closed four of seven military bases in Chiapas, released rebel prisoners and submitted an indigenous rights bill to Congress for approval. Marcos and a handful of Zapatista rebels left their hiding place in the mountains in March 2001 and led a two-week caravan, dubbed the Zapatour by the media, to Mexico City to demand passage of the Indian rights bill. One hundred thousand supporters attended a demonstration to greet the Zapatistas. The political debate floundered, however, and it became clear that a resolution would not come easily. Congress passed the indigenous rights bill but made so many changes that the Zapatistas rejected it as unacceptable.

The Zapatistas have a website, and their cause has gained sympathy among people around the world who oppose the globalized economy that Mexico's government is pursuing. The rebels represent not only Mexico's poor, illiterate, indigenous peoples, but also small farmers and manual labourers who do not enjoy the benefits of global trade.

President Fox has not found it easy to make all the changes he promised. His party does not have a majority in Congress, economic

Vicente Fox, the first non-PRI candidate to be elected president of Mexico since 1929, took office in 2000.

problems persist and people who benefited under the old regime are fighting hard to resist the new order. For the first time, Mexico is openly tied to the United States, both economically and politically – a stance that has generated some criticism. Fox also hopes that he and the US president can find a solution to the serious problem of illegal immigration of Mexicans into the United States. Despite these challenges, many people support Fox and the changes he is bringing to his country.

Government

The United Mexican States, commonly called Mexico, is a federal republic consisting of thirty-one states and a federal district, where Mexico City is located. The president, who is elected for one six-year term, holds executive power. He appoints a cabinet that directs government operations. The president has tremendous influence over the government, and each Mexican president has placed a very strong personal imprint on his administration.

The legislative branch of government consists of a congress with an upper chamber (the Senate) and a lower chamber (the Chamber of Deputies). The Senate has 128 members, elected for six-year terms. The five hundred members of the Chamber of Deputies are elected for three-year terms. In the judicial branch, the Supreme Court of Justice is the highest court in the country.

Each state has its own constitution and is administered by a governor, elected for a six-year term and a legislature. All adults aged eighteen and over are eligible to vote.

THE PEOPLE

A Diverse People

Mexico is the largest Spanish-speaking country in the world, with a population of nearly 100 million. That population is growing rapidly, since the majority of Mexicans are still children or young adults.

Mexico has made a serious effort to control population growth, and the rate of growth declined steadily between 1965 and 1997. Nevertheless, the population is expected to increase to 130.9 million by 2025, as the country's large numbers of young people start having families of their own. Between 2001 and 2050, the Mexican population is projected to increase by 50 per cent.

More than 450 years after the Spaniards conquered the Aztecs, Mexico has become a unique blend of indigenous and European peoples. About 60 per cent of Mexicans are mestizo, with the dark skin and eyes of their native ancestors and the language and Catholic religion of Spain. Most Mexican culture is a mixture of both native and imported traditions.

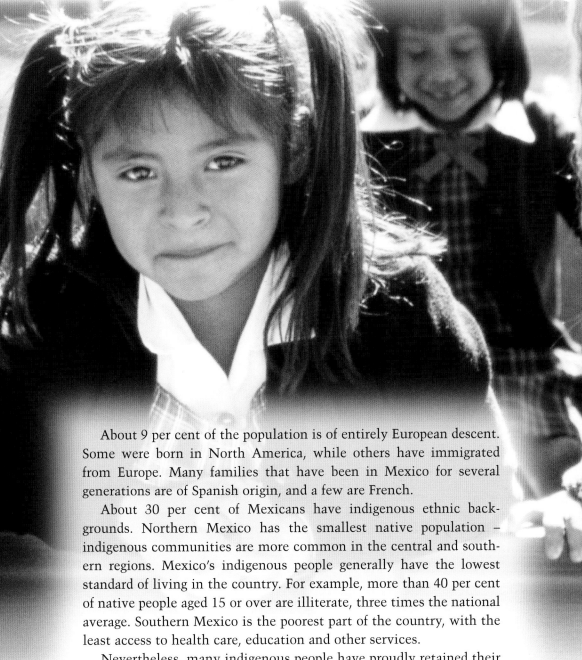

About 9 per cent of the population is of entirely European descent. Some were born in North America, while others have immigrated from Europe. Many families that have been in Mexico for several generations are of Spanish origin, and a few are French.

About 30 per cent of Mexicans have indigenous ethnic backgrounds. Northern Mexico has the smallest native population – indigenous communities are more common in the central and southern regions. Mexico's indigenous people generally have the lowest standard of living in the country. For example, more than 40 per cent of native people aged 15 or over are illiterate, three times the national average. Southern Mexico is the poorest part of the country, with the least access to health care, education and other services.

Nevertheless, many indigenous people have proudly retained their traditions. They speak their languages on a daily basis, participate in religious ceremonies that are rooted in ancient traditions and try to live in harmony with nature.

Voladores perform a traditional pole dance during a celebration in El Tajin, Mexico.

VOLADORES

Indigenous cultures remain strong in Mexico. During fiestas (festivals), native dancers wear traditional costumes and perform regional dances. They may also perform ceremonies such as the Voladores, in which several men climb to the top of a high pole, then soar to the ground, suspended from ropes, circling the pole thirteen times as they descend. The ceremony is mostly performed for tourists, but has roots in the religious beliefs of the Totonac people.

Some 5.3 million Mexicans speak an indigenous language. More than ninety native languages are spoken, some by only a handful of people. The most common is Nahuátl, the language of the Aztecs, whose descendants are known as the Nahua people. Other languages include Maya, Mixtec, Zapotec, Otomí, Tzeltal and Tzotzil.

Maya is heard in the Yucatán Peninsula, where 44 per cent of residents speak the language, as well as in Chiapas. The region with the greatest linguistic diversity is Oaxaca, where twelve different Indian languages are spoken.

Improvements in health care in the mid-twentieth century led to a population explosion. By 1970 the population of Mexico had reached 48.2 million, climbing from 20 million in 1940. Concerned about the rapid population growth, government officials set up a family planning programme that encourages responsible parenthood and offers family planning counselling to women. This programme has been very successful, and the birth rate, or average number of children born to a woman during her lifetime, has fallen from a high of 3.5 in 1970 to 2.7. This falls between the rate of 3.1 for countries of Central America and 2.1 for the United States of America.

A Young, Urban Population

Most Mexicans are young. According to government statistics for the year 2000, about one-third of the population, or 32.6 million Mexicans, were aged 14 and under, and another 10 million were between 15 and 19. There were 17.2 million people between the ages of 20 and 29, and 13.5 million between the ages of 30 and 39. About 17.4 million were between 40 and 64, and only 4.7 million were 65 years old and over.

The scarcity of jobs, services and farmland in rural Mexico means that at least 70 per cent of the population lives in urban areas. The cities and fertile farmland of the Mesa Central are the country's hub. In 2000 the state of México had 13 million inhabitants and the Federal District (the heart of Mexico City) had 8.6 million. Nearby Puebla state had 5 million inhabitants and Guanajuato had 4.6 million people.

Young people, like these enthusiastic teenage football fans, make up a large part of the Mexican population. One in three Mexicans is aged 15 or younger.

Baja California Sur is the least populated state, with only 423,000 inhabitants, while border industrial cities like Tijuana and Ciudad Juárez are the fastest-growing regions. The rapid growth has put a huge strain on these cities, which cannot keep up with the demand for services such as water, sewers and housing.

A significant proportion of Mexicans do not live in Mexico at all, but live and work in the United States, often illegally. These undocumented workers risk deportation for the sake of higher wages in the United States.

Health

Mexico has both public and private health care systems, although private hospitals and doctors have a better reputation. People who work for large companies or the government – the so-called formal sector of the economy – receive government-subsidized health care benefits through a social security programme. Mexicans who work in the informal sector, such as the city street vendors, are also supposed to receive health care from govern-ment agencies, but there are fewer doctors and hospitals to serve their needs. Access to

Street vendor

health care also varies by region. Mexico City and some northern states have the best facilities and care, while the southern states score badly. Many villages have clinics staffed by nurses, but people have to go to a larger city for anything more than basic health care. Rural areas, especially regions with large indigenous populations, have lower health standards than cities. Health and san-itation services are also much worse in urban slums.

Overall, however, progress has been made. The likelihood that a Mexican child will die before age five has decreased dramatically since 1960. Mexico's infant mortality

Drug abuse is a growing health and social problem, especially in border cities such as Tijuana. There, a government study found that about 15 per cent of the population had tried drugs, such as methamphetamines, at least once. Tijuana has several drug treatment centres, but the city is a major stop on the drug smuggling route between Colombia and the United States. In all of Mexico, less than 1 per cent of people are addicted to drugs, while 25 per cent use tobacco and 9.4 per cent abuse alcohol.

Many Mexicans, such as this indigenous woman from Oaxaca, are living into their seventies, thanks to advances in health care and improved living conditions.

rate – the number of infant deaths per 1,000 births – is 31.5. This is lower than the South and Central American averages of 34, but far above the US infant mortality rate of 7. The average Mexican lives to age 72. In 1960 the average life expectancy was only 48.1 years for men and 51 for women.

The leading causes of death in Mexico are typical of industrialized countries: heart disease, cancer and diabetes. But at the beginning of the twenty-first century, almost 10,000 deaths were attributed to malnutrition and other dietary deficiencies. Another 5,600 deaths were caused by intestinal diseases, reflecting poor sanitation. Access to safe water is not available to 17 per cent of the population, and 23 per cent lacks adequate sanitation.

Almost 20,000 people died of chronic lung diseases – bronchitis, emphysema and asthma – in Mexico at the end of the twentieth century. Bad air quality is a likely factor. The United Nations estimates that about 150,000 Mexican adults and children were living with HIV/AIDS at the beginning of the twenty-first century. About 14,000 children in Mexico have been orphaned since the epidemic began. Estimates of adult deaths from AIDS range from 4,200 to 7,400.

Education

According to government figures, 89 per cent of Mexicans aged fifteen and over can read. Literacy rates are higher among young people than the elderly.

The government has strived to improve the quality of education and reduce dropout rates. It has built many new schools and changed the law to require children to stay in school until they are aged fourteen (rather than aged eleven). The law has not been very successful, since hundreds of thousands of young Mexicans never even complete primary school.

Many Mexican families move from villages to big cities because education in rural schools is so poor. Primary schools in rural areas often have only one teacher and don't even go up to grade six, and the closest secondary school may be hours away.

Children attend pre-school, nursery school and six years of primary school. For those who continue, secondary school lasts three years. Some students go into vocational programmes after their primary education.

After secondary school, a three-year college preparatory programme is available, as is advanced technical training. There are more than fifty universities in Mexico, many with campuses in several cities, as well as technological institutes and teacher-training colleges. The largest university is the National Autonomous University of Mexico in Mexico City, with an enrolment of more than one hundred thousand students. Some universities offer graduate courses, but research opportunities are limited and many young people study in other countries.

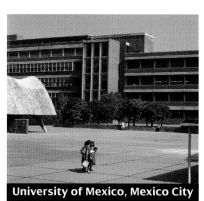

University of Mexico, Mexico City

Primary students in a Mexico City school wrestle with exam questions.

Most schools and universities are public, but families who can afford it may choose to send their children to private schools. The federal government ran the public system until 1993, when responsibility for education was given to the states. Educators hoped that the states would make schooling more relevant to local needs, reduce bureaucracy and spend more money on training teachers and improving resources. The curriculum was changed, with an emphasis on basic reading, writing and maths.

 To learn more about the indigenous peoples of Mexico – including the Maya, Olmecs, Zapotecs and other ethnic groups – the most up-to-date population figures; the most current health statistics; and other current demographic statistics for Mexico, go to vgsbooks.com for links.

CULTURAL LIFE

Just as the land is a tapestry of mountains, jungles and deserts, Mexico's culture blends many influences, old and new, European and indigenous. Spanish traditions have shaped the country's language, religion and architecture. Indigenous cultures are seen in the arts and cuisine, and their presence is strongest in rural areas where people remain more isolated.

The Tarahumara Indians of Chihuahua speak a language related to that of the Apaches of the south-western United States. The Tarahumaras have preserved much of their ancient culture and are especially knowledgeable about the medicinal uses of plants and herbs. They are famed for their speed and endurance as long-distance runners, abilities they originally developed as hunters chasing deer.

The Huichols of the Sierra Madre Occidental still practise the religious ceremonies of their ancestors, including the use of the hallucinogenic peyote cactus. They also are admired for their yarn paintings, weaving, embroidery and beadwork.

The Maya live in southern Chiapas state and the Yucatán Peninsula, where they speak thirty-five different versions of the Maya language. Most Maya are farmers. Each extended family lives in a compound made up of several single-room buildings built around a private, open-air patio.

▶ Religion

More than 90 per cent of Mexicans are Roman Catholic, and about 3 per cent are members of various Protestant and Evangelical churches. The Catholic Church plays an important role in Mexican family life, from baptisms to funerals. A child's first Communion, usually around the age of eleven, is an important day.

Many fiestas, or festivals, celebrate religious occasions. Easter week, for example, brings Passion plays, palm leaves and processions throughout the country. The feast day of the Virgin of Guadalupe is celebrated on 12 December. On 15 August, the Feast of the

Assumption, people in some towns carry a religious statue through flower-strewn streets.

Although most indigenous people are officially Catholic, many also observe their ancestral religious customs. For example, some farmers ask the rain god to send rain for their crops, while others sacrifice roosters to ensure the soil's fertility.

Religion and medicine also fuse in some areas, where people ask healers to use special herbs and foods, along with prayer to the Catholic saints, to cure illness. Many Indians believe that people can hurt others by giving them the evil eye, and that only a healer can cure someone who has been harmed in this way.

◉ Architecture and Art

The Maya, Aztecs, and other indigenous peoples were Mexico's first architects. The remains of their stone pyramids and carvings stand as monuments to their genius and continue to inspire Mexican artists.

Religion, art and architecture come together in Mexico's thirteen thousand religious buildings. Colonial churches were influenced by various European styles. Many have altars covered in gold, and some are decorated with colourful tiles and show other influences from southern Spain. The baroque style was popular in the 1600s, featuring multitudes of plaster angels, saints and flowers. Some churches built after 1750 were designed

A mural by Diego Rivera, a visual artist whose work frequently explores political themes, depicts the cruelty of Spanish colonial rule through a scene of slavery on a sugar plantation in Tealtenango, Morelos.

in an extremely ornate style, which is unique to Latin America, called churrigueresque.

During the colonial era, Spanish missionaries tried to teach Indians the messages of the Bible by decorating church walls with brightly coloured frescoes (paintings on plaster) of religious scenes. Native artisans did a lot of the work, therefore the Christian symbols are mixed with indigenous themes, as in carved angels covered with feathers to resemble the Aztec god Quetzalcóatl.

Mexico's best-known modern artists are the mural painters Diego Rivera, José Clemente Orozco and David Alfaro Siqueiros. They were hired by the government after the 1921 revolution to portray Mexican history on public buildings. Their murals glorified the cultures of the past and were inspired by the artists' left-wing political beliefs.

Mexico's most renowned female artist, Frida Kahlo, is revered for her vivid self-portraits and politically themed works. Kahlo, also the wife of Diego Rivera, was strongly influenced by Mexican folk art.

Mexico is also famous for its crafts, such as intricate silver jewellery, blue and white tiles, hand-painted pottery vases, and carved wooden spoons and toys. Some of the textiles are still coloured using traditional dyes made from plant and insect sources. Masks representing people, supernatural beings, birds, and animals are made for fiestas and special ceremonies.

Literature and Language

Spanish is the official language of Mexico. However, more than fifty indigenous languages are also used throughout the country.

Mexican literary traditions go back to pre-colonial times. The Maya had an elaborate writing system and recorded their history in stone carvings, as well as in accordion-folded books called codices. The Aztecs had a pictograph writing system, but most Aztec stories were preserved through oral storytelling. Many indigenous myths explained the natural world – seasons, the creation of the universe and geographical features.

The first book written by a European about Mexico was *The True History of the Conquest of New Spain* by Bernal Díaz del Castillo, a Spanish soldier who accompanied Cortés and described the conquistadors' encounters with indigenous people. In 1816 José Joaquín Fernández de Lizardi published *The Itching Parrot*, believed to be the first Latin American novel.

Among contemporary writers, Mexico's two intellectual giants are Nobel Prize-winning poet Octavio Paz and novelist and essayist Carlos Fuentes. Laura Esquivel is well known for her novel *Like Water for Chocolate*, which was made into a successful movie.

Carlos Fuentes

Most Mexicans, however, lack strong reading skills. The most popular reading materials in the urban slums are newspapers featuring stories about violent crime, drugs and corruption, and comic-book-style novels, illustrated with photographs of actors, that tell tales of romance and betrayal.

Media

Several television networks operate in Mexico, including the private Televisa and Azteca networks and the state-run IMEVISION, which shows cultural and scientific programmes. The networks have been criticized for showing too many US programmes.

Mexico has about seven hundred commercial radio stations. There are also many newspapers, especially in Mexico City, where eight large daily newspapers cover the news.

The golden age of Mexican film-making was the mid-1930s to the mid-1950s. In 2001 *Amores Perros* was nominated in the United States for an Academy Award as best foreign-language film.

Musicians play at a mariachi festival. Mariachi music has been popular in Mexico for nearly two hundred years.

Music and Dance

Mexican music ranges from traditional Indian rhythms, played on reed flutes, shells and seedpods, to modern symphony orchestras. The guitar, introduced by the Spanish, is very popular. Guitars, along with violins and trumpets, form the mariachi bands that can be heard at celebrations everywhere. The mariachi tradition is said to have originated in the state of Jalisco during the 1800s, when small bands played at the weddings of French soldiers to Mexican women. The word *mariachi* comes from the French word for marriage.

Country and western music is popular in Mexico, where it is called *norteño*, or ranchero music. Norteño groups usually use an accordion and a guitar, while the singer keeps the beat with drumsticks on a piece of wood.

Some Mexican pop stars have achieved fame beyond Mexico. Grammy-winner Luis Miguel began his career in the 1980s as a teen star and grew up to be a sophisticated crooner. Los Tigres del Norte have become working-class heroes with their *corridos*, or urban border, music about Mexicans living in the United States.

Dance has helped preserve Mexico's indigenous heritage, and no fiesta would be complete without dancers wearing costumes that reflect local traditions. The *jarabe tapatío*, or Mexican hat dance, performed around a large sombrero, is the national folk dance. The Ballet Folklorico de México performs many of these dances for audiences at home and abroad.

Many handicrafts created for Day of the Dead celebrations, such as these festive paper dolls, depict smiling skeletons or skulls. During this late autumn holiday, Mexicans attempt to commune with their deceased ancestors. Go to vgsbooks.com if you'd like to learn more about el Día de los Muertos.

◉ Holidays

Mexicans mark more than a dozen national holidays every year. Some holidays have historical significance, while others stem from religious faith. Many holidays are celebrated with fiestas featuring parades, music, dancing, fireworks and fairs, where artisans and vendors set up stalls to sell their goods.

Legal holidays include Christmas Day, New Year's Day, Good Friday and Labour Day. Constitution Day is 5 February, and the birthday of Benito Juárez is celebrated on 21 March. Cinco de Mayo (5 May) remembers the defeat of French invaders near Puebla in 1862.

Mexico's biggest national holiday is Independence Day, which recalls the event in 1810 that began the country's fight for freedom from Spanish rule. Just as Father Hidalgo called his parishioners together then, each year on 15 September the president of Mexico steps onto the balcony of the National Palace and rings the same church bell the priest used. Then he repeats some of Father Hidalgo's speech. When he waves the flag and cries, 'Mexicanos, que viva México!' (Mexicans, long live Mexico!), the crowd below answers,

'Viva!'. Fireworks, music and a huge fiesta follow.

On Day of the Dead, celebrated 31 October through to 2 November, Mexicans follow a centuries-old tradition of trying to communicate with deceased friends and relatives. Far from being morbid or scary, this is a peaceful occasion. In some towns, people light small fires near their front doors to help guide the deceased to their families. Other people use bright yellow flowers or candles to light the way. Some families visit the graveyard, where they sing the dead person's favourite songs, or they make an altar to the deceased at home, surrounding it with the loved one's favourite foods.

A growing number of Mexican children also celebrate Halloween, a holiday imported from the United States. Some people worry that the commercialism of Halloween will overshadow the Day of the Dead.

In many homes, Christmas celebrations start with a *posada*, a party held sometime during the nine days before Christmas. A girl and boy play the roles of Mary and Joseph. As they look for a place to stay, the children and other guests go to three houses. They are turned away from the first two, but at the third house, they are invited in and the party begins. The guests drink *ponche* (a hot fruit drink) and listen to music, while the children take turns trying to break open a *piñata* filled with fruit and sweets.

Mexican Food

Mexican food is world famous for its tacos, tortillas and enchiladas, but these are just a small part of the cuisine. Mexican food is very diverse. Different regions have their own specialities and distinctive flavours, and not all the food is spicy hot.

In addition to the corn, beans and squash that were the staples of their diet, the ancient people of Mexico learned to cultivate a number of wild plants, including avocados, chilli peppers, tomatoes, cacao, sunflowers, papaya, mushrooms and vanilla. The Spaniards introduced rice, olives, lemons, grapes, sugar cane, beef, pork and various spices and herbs to Mexican cuisine.

Chocolate comes from the seed pods of the tropical cacao tree, native to Mexico and Central America. The Maya prized chocolate, which they made into a beverage drunk at ceremonies such as weddings. The Aztecs used cacao beans as a form of currency. They also prepared a chocolate beverage by toasting and grinding the beans into powder. Flavoured with spices, vanilla, honey or flowers, this drink was enjoyed by royalty and used in religious rituals.

Maize is thought to have been farmed in Mexico as early as 5000 BC. Usually it is ground and boiled, then made into dough. The dough is flattened into tortillas and wrapped around a variety of fillings. Corn tortillas are most popular in southern Mexico, while wheat tortillas are more common in the north. *Tamales* are dumplings made with corn dough, filled with meat and chilli sauce, then wrapped in corn husks or banana leaves and steamed.

Tamale vendor

A great variety of chilli peppers are grown in Mexico. Chillies may be stuffed with meat or cheese, or they may be diced and put in a sauce. In the Oaxaca region, people make seven basic types of sauce with different kinds of chilli peppers, along with other ingredients such as avocado leaves, banana, pineapple or string beans. *Mole poblano*, which originated near Puebla in colonial times, is known as Mexico's national dish. It is turkey with a chilli, nut and chocolate sauce.

Many Mexicans eat their main meal in the middle of the day. It usually includes soup, salad, rice and a main course with beans, tortillas and vegetables. Dessert and coffee follow. Flan, or caramel custard, is the most popular dessert.

MEXICAN HOT CHOCOLATE

Mexican chocolate is available in the form of round, flat, cinnamon-flavoured tablets. It is used to make hot cocoa. If you can't find Mexican chocolate, use sweet cooking chocolate.

170 g of Mexican or sweet cooking chocolate

1.4 litres milk

1½ tsp cinnamon (if you are using cooking chocolate)

1. Combine the ingredients in a saucepan and cook slowly over low heat, stirring constantly until the chocolate has melted and blended into the milk. Remove from heat.

2. Use a hand-operated whisk to beat the chocolate until it is frothy. Serve in a large pottery jug for an authentic Mexican touch.

Sport

Mexico's national passion is *fútbol,* or football. Every small town has a football pitch and competitions are organized between schools, factories and other groups. The professional league has dozens of teams. The most popular are from Mexico City and Guadalajara. The Azteca Stadium in Mexico City, which can hold one hundred thousand screaming fans, has hosted World Cup football finals several times.

Béisbol, or baseball, introduced from the United States of America, is also very popular. Children play at school or in leagues and professional teams compete in the Caribbean World Series.

Adults and children alike play fast-paced jai alai in a three-walled court using a hard rubber ball and long-handled wicker scoops. Some people like to bet on the outcome of games.

The Spaniards brought bullfighting to Mexico, and Mexico City boasts the largest bullfighting arena in the world, the Plaza de Toros, which holds up to sixty thousand people. Bullfights take place between November and April, usually on Sunday afternoons. Matadors, dressed in silver- and gold-sequinned costumes, are admired for their courage and talent. The matador has sixteen minutes to kill the bull, or else the fight is over. While matadors are occasionally injured or killed, the bull usually loses.

Charreadas, events similar to rodeos, are popular, especially in ranching areas. Cowboys, called *charros,* show off their skills in lassoing and bull riding. The charro's traditional costume includes tight pants, a short jacket, bow tie and an embroidered sombrero.

A matador and bull confront each other in a Cancun bullfighting ring.

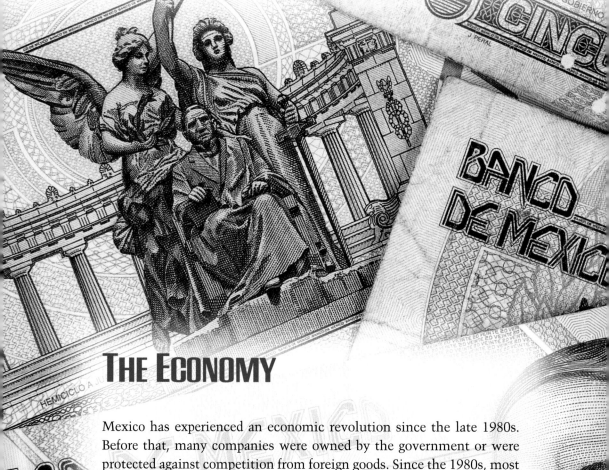

THE ECONOMY

Mexico has experienced an economic revolution since the late 1980s. Before that, many companies were owned by the government or were protected against competition from foreign goods. Since the 1980s, most Mexican businesses have been owned by private investors, and the country has embraced free trade, taking its place as an industrialized nation in a global economy. Its economy strengthened steadily during the late 1990s. Gross domestic product, a key measure of economic productivity, increased by 7 per cent in 2000.

One reason for Mexico's growing economic strength is the North American Free Trade Agreement (NAFTA) with the United States and Canada. In effect since 1994, NAFTA is gradually dismantling trade barriers. As a result, Mexico has replaced Japan as the United States's second biggest trading partner after Canada.

Mexico has signed trade agreements with Chile, Costa Rica and several other Central and South American countries. Free trade agreements with Israel and the fifteen-member European Union came into

effect in 2000, and Mexico signed an agreement with the European Free Trade Association, a group of four non-European-Union members.

Free trade is central to Mexico's economic strategy, but some people are concerned that the trade agreements put corporations ahead of countries. They worry, for example, that the agreements undermine countries' abilities to enforce environmental protection laws. Mexico's principal exports include vehicles and automotive parts, telecommunications and sound equipment, crude petroleum and petroleum products, chemicals, clothing and fruit and vegetables.

Manufacturing, Oil and Mining

In the mid-1960s, Mexico launched a programme that set aside a twenty-kilometre-wide (12-mile-wide) industrial strip along the US border. In this zone, any foreign (primarily US) company can set up a manufacturing plant called a *maquiladora*. For example, a US toaster-maker can import parts from the United States, have them assembled by low-paid Mexican workers, then ship the toasters to shops in the United States of America. The company pays no duty, or import tax, just a small tax on the value added to the product during the manufacturing process. The programme has been very successful, accounting for most foreign investment in Mexico. The main products produced along the border are cars, electronics, furniture, chemicals and textiles.

About 22 per cent of Mexican workers are employed in maquiladoras and other industries. Most factories are in Mexico City, Guadalajara, Monterrey and other northern cities. Manufactured products include beer, cigarettes, household appliances, cement, tyres, cars and vans. Other important industries include processing sugar cane, wheat flour and corn flour as well as making iron and steel.

Mexico is the fifth largest petroleum-exporting country in the world. Oil contributes significantly to the country's income, although the world price of oil fluctuates. Petróleos Mexicanos (PEMEX) has a monopoly over petroleum and gas exploration and distribution. This industry employs less than 1 per cent of Mexico's workers.

Petroleum mining helps form the backbone of the Mexican economy. This oil rig is located in the Gulf of Mexico.

Manufacturing plants, such as this cement factory in Guanajuato State, provide jobs to a fifth of Mexico's workforce.

Mexico is the world's leading silver producer and the seventh largest copper producer. Many other resources are mined, including gold, lead, zinc, iron, sulphur and coal.

Service Industries

Half of the official labour force in Mexico works in service industries, including health and social services, banking, business services, government and hotels. Tourism is an important source of foreign currency. Most tourists come from the United States of America to visit Mexico City and beach resorts along the Pacific and Yucatán coasts. More than ten million tourists stayed in Mexico in 1998 (not counting those who crossed the border for only a day), injecting more than $5 billion into the economy.

Many Mexicans work in the so-called informal economy. These are street vendors, taxi drivers and others who are basically self-employed. Many of these workers avoid paying taxes on their income.

Agriculture

Although 27 per cent of the labour force works in agriculture, farming represents only about 5 per cent of Mexico's economy. The principal crops are corn, wheat, sorghum (a grain used as animal fodder) and sugarcane. Cattle are the most numerous livestock, followed by pigs, goats, sheep and horses. Poultry are also raised.

Agriculture, especially in the south of Mexico, is still very labour intensive. Not only are farmers unable to afford modern farm machinery that would make their jobs easier, but also most farms are not large enough to accommodate large equipment such as tractors. Many

In the rich sandy soil of northern Mexico, many kinds of chillies grow very well. Harvesting by hand is still common, as many farmers cannot afford modern equipment.

ejidos (communal landholdings) do not produce enough maize and beans even to feed a family. Large commercial farms produce fruit and vegetables, such as oranges, apples, bananas, mangoes, melons, tomatoes, chillies and strawberries.

Forestry is not as important to the economy as it was in the past, since so many trees have been logged. Some logging continues to provide wood for firewood, construction materials, furniture and paper products. Commercial fishing occurs primarily on the Gulf Coast, where shrimp and sardines are caught.

Infrastructure

Mexico has more than 320,000 km (200,000 miles) of roads, including about 50,000 km (30,000 miles) of motorways, but many roads in the south are narrow, muddy and dangerous. Goods are transported primarily by lorry.

Mexico City has a large underground train system, and Guadalajara and Monterrey have commuter trains. There is a large international airport in Mexico City and more than eighty other international and domestic airports in the rest of the country. The most important ports include Tampico, Veracruz and Coatzacoalcos on the Gulf Coast and Salina Cruz and Manzanillo on the Pacific.

Mexicans have more television sets than telephones. About eleven million telephone lines operate in Mexico. Almost all telephone service is provided by Telmex, which was privatized in 1991.

Mexico produces three-quarters of its electricity from fossil fuels –

coal, oil or natural gas, while hydroelectricity contributes about 20 per cent of the nation's electricity. The rest of the power comes from nuclear plants and other sources.

Economic Challenges

Despite its growing economy, Mexico faces many challenges. With its young and growing population, the country needs to provide better education and training to produce skilled workers and professionals. The economy has not created enough jobs, especially well-paid ones. Many people cross the border illegally into the United States to find work. Every day, about 4,600 people are caught trying to cross the border. Out of 2000 people more than 400 people died of exposure or drowned in the attempt. In May 2001, a group of Mexicans paid a smuggler (called a 'coyote') to guide them across the border into Arizona. After five days of wandering in the scorching heat of the desert, fourteen of the immigrants died. This incident sparked both humanitarian efforts to help future immigrants cross safely and examination of border policies by Mexican and US officials.

About five million Mexicans, many with trade or professional skills, live and work illegally in the United States. They send approximately $6 billion home each year, a huge contribution to the Mexican economy. In one small Mexican town, where drought caused the maize crop to fail for three years, money from family members working in the United States paid for a new water system, medical clinic and schools. Many families have paid for new homes with this income. However, talented people who could be contributing to their own communities are absent for much of the year, and families are separated.

This situation has created friction between Mexico and the United States. The two governments have discussed starting a guest-worker programme, in which Mexican workers would be allowed to stay temporarily in the United States to meet US employment needs. If the proposal is approved, Mexicans could travel freely across the border and receive US Social Security and other benefits.

Drug trafficking is another source of tension between Mexico and the US. President Fox has promised to wage a serious offensive against drug traffickers. In one case, a former Mexican state governor and police officer faced charges of shipping tonnes of cocaine from Colombia to the United States. Mexicans also collaborated with US and Colombian authorities to break up a network that had smuggled millions of dollars' worth of cocaine and marijuana through Nuevo Laredo, Mexico.

Another serious challenge for Mexico is to close the gap between the very rich and the desperately poor. The poorest 40 per cent of households receive 12 per cent of total household income, while the wealthiest 20 per cent receive 55 per cent of total household income. In 2001 the government introduced a new programme to make small business loans available to people who had not previously had access to loans for projects such as repair shops, home sewing businesses or street-corner sweet stands.

Because of NAFTA, Mexican employees of companies making goods for export can earn comparatively good wages. Maquiladoras workers making staplers, for example, made ten dollars a day in 2000, more than double the minimum wage of four dollars a day. In contrast, many Mexicans still earned only two or three dollars a day selling trinkets on the street or doing unskilled jobs.

The middle class also needs to be strengthened. Although many Mexican people earn better wages than ever before, they still run into problems. It is extremely difficult to borrow money to buy a house or car or to start or improve a small business. After the 1994 economic collapse, most banks stopped making consumer loans except to the very rich.

An equally crucial challenge will be to bring the relatively prosperous, industrialized north and the poor south closer together economically. In 2001 the government announced a programme to improve the infrastructure and encourage business development in the south.

Mexico is also susceptible to economic setbacks from natural disasters such as earthquakes and hurricanes. Agriculture is hampered by drought, especially in northern areas, where industries and farmers compete for water supplies that are quickly being depleted. The economy suffers from environmental destruction, including the loss of forests and the pollution of fishing grounds by the petroleum industry.

Visit vgsbooks.com for links to websites with additional information on Mexico's economy, a conversion programme that provides the most up-to-date exchange rate, in-depth coverage of Mexico's relationship with the United States, and detailed information on NAFTA.

ⓞ Conclusion

In 2000, with the election of Vicente Fox, Mexico made a giant leap towards full democracy. It has new institutions, such as a human rights commission, and the courts and media are less dependent on the government than in the past.

President Fox has promised Mexicans open government, human rights, continued economic growth and an attack on poverty. During his six-year-term he urged the United States government to be more lenient towards Mexican immigration. Vicente was unable to run for a second term, and in 2006 his successor Felipe Calderon won a narrow victory over the left-wing candidate Andres Manuel Lopez Obrador.

Vicente Fox

After his election Calderon offered to include opposition politicians in his government. Two major problems for him to tackle are the continued and persistent poverty and the fight against the powerful drug cartels.

Mexico's manufactured exports, oil exports and foreign investment depend heavily on the United States, which has experienced an economic slowdown in recent years. Mexico's economic growth has slowed as a result.

Mexican leaders are seeking a more assertive role in world affairs and now show more confidence in their relationship with the United States. However many Mexicans worry that their ancient traditions could be overwhelmed by American popular culture. Time will tell if the new government of Felipe Calderon is able rise to the challenge.

Timeline

c 12,000 BC	Hunters and gatherers live in the area that is present-day Mexico.
c 7000 BC	Agriculture begins in Mexico.
c 1500 BC	Villages appear. Inhabitants produce clay products.
c 1200–400 BC	The Olmec culture flourishes.
c 600 BC	The first settlement in Mexico is established at Monte Albán.
c AD 300–900	Classic Maya civilization spreads throughout central and southern Mexico.
c 400–650	The Teotihuacán culture dominates central Mexico.
c 600–1520	Mixtecs dominate south-central Mexico.
c 900	Zapotecs abandon Monte Albán.
c 900–1200	The Toltec empire flourishes.
c 1300	Aztecs found Tenochtitlán.
1502	Moctezuma II becomes Aztec emperor.
1519	Hernán Cortés lands near Veracruz.
1521	Spaniards take over Tenochtitlán, and Mexico falls to the conquistadors. The Spanish Colonial period begins.
1531	Juan Diego sees a vision of the Virgin Mary, which becomes known as the Virgin of Guadalupe.
1536	Mexico's first printing press opens in Mexico City.
1810	Father Miguel Hidalgo issues a call for independence.
1811	Father Hidalgo is executed.
1821	The Treaty of Córdoba recognizes Mexico as an independent nation.
1836	Texas declares independence from Mexico. Battle of the Alamo takes place in March.
1846	The Mexican-American War begins.
1847	The United States of America invades Mexico.
1848	The Treaty of Guadalupe Hidalgo ends the Mexican-American War, resulting in loss of large territory for Mexico.
1857	President Benito Juárez and reformers introduce a liberal constitution.

1858–1861	The War of the Reform takes place between liberals and conservatives.
1862	Mexican forces defeat French invaders on 5 May near Puebla.
1864–1867	The French-backed Emperor Maximilian I rules Mexico.
1876–1911	Porfirio Diaz maintains a dictatorship, known as the Porfiriato.
1910–1920	Mexican Revolution takes place.
1919	Emiliano Zapata is assassinated.
1929	The forerunner of the PRI is founded.
1929–1935	Artist Diego Rivera paints a mural around the staircase of the National Palace in Mexico City
1934	The Palacio de Bellas Artes in Mexico City is completed.
1938	Mexico's oil industry is nationalized.
1945	Mexico becomes a charter member of the United Nations.
1953	Mexican women gain the right to vote and hold elected office.
1968	The summer Olympics are held in Mexico City and protesters are killed at Tlatelolco Plaza.
1982	Economic crisis begins.
1985	An earthquake kills at least 9,500 people in Mexico City.
1988	Carlos Salinas de Gortari is elected president.
1990	Octavio Paz wins the Nobel Prize for literature.
1994	NAFTA takes effect; Chiapas rebellion breaks out.
2000	Vicente Fox is elected president.
2001	Chiapas rebels go to Mexico City to support the passage of an Indian rights bill.
2002	Vicente Fox and US president George W. Bush meet to discuss trade and immigration issues related to the Mexican-United States border.
2006	A new federal police force is created to tackle drug cartels. Felipe Calderon wins presidential election.
2007	Heavy rain floods parts of Mexico. Some 500,000 are made homeless in one of the country's worst natural disasters.

COUNTRY NAME United Mexican States

AREA 1,923,040 square kilometres (742,489 square miles).

MAIN LANDFORMS Mexican Plateau, Sierra Madre Occidental, Sierra Madre Oriental, Cordillera Neo-Volcánica, Gulf Coastal Plain, Chiapas Highlands, Sierra Madre del Sur, Pacific Coastal Lowlands, Baja California Peninsula

HIGHEST POINT Pico de Orizaba (Orizaba peak), 5,700 metres above sea level

LOWEST POINT Near Mexicali, 10 metres below sea level

MAJOR RIVERS Bravo del Norte, Panuco, Lerma, Balsas

ANIMALS Desert bighorn sheep, grey whales, jaguars, quetzals, Gila monsters

CAPITAL CITY Mexico City

OTHER MAJOR CITIES Guadalajara, Puebla, Monterrey

OFFICIAL LANGUAGE Spanish

MONETARY UNIT Peso. 100 centavos = 1 peso

MEXICO'S CURRENCY

Mexico's monetary unit is the peso, with 100 centavos in a peso. When Mexico was founded, the peso was the currency of Spain, and Mexico retained the peso after becoming independent. The first Mexican-minted peso appeared in 1536. The currency was revalued in 1993, with 1 new peso equal to 1,000 old pesos. The one-peso coin has a stainless steel edge and an aluminium/bronze centre. It bears the image of an eagle perched on a cactus. Peso coins come in denominations of 1, 2, 5, 10 and 20, and paper currency denominations are 10, 20, 50, 100, 200 and 500 pesos.

Mexico's flag and national anthem date from the independence era. The green, white and red flag was officially adopted in 1823. The colours represent hope (green), purity (white) and blood (red).

At the centre is an eagle, perched on a cactus and holding a rattlesnake. This symbol stems from the legend about the Aztec people who founded Tenochtitlán (later Mexico City) on an island where they saw such an eagle.

The red fruit of the prickly pear cactus also has a place on the flag. It symbolized the human heart to the Aztecs. A garland, or open crown of branches, surrounds the eagle. On the left are oak branches, symbolizing strength, while the right side has laurel branches to signify victory.

The 'Himno Nacional Mexicano' was first played on Independence Day in 1854, after a national contest to choose an anthem. The patriotic words are by Francisco González Bocanegra, set to music by Jaime Nunó. Here is the chorus and first verse:

Mexicans, when the war cry is heard,
Have sword and bridle ready.
Let the earth's foundations tremble
At the loud cannon's roar.

May the divine archangel crown your brow,
O fatherland, with an olive branch of peace,
For your eternal destiny has been written
In heaven by the finger of God.
But should a foreign enemy
Dare to profane your soil with his tread,
Know, beloved fatherland, that heaven gave you
A soldier in each of your sons.

 For a link to a site where you can listen to an instrumental version of Mexico's national anthem, go to vgsbooks.com.

CARLOS CHÁVEZ (1899–1978) Born in Mexico City, Chávez is one of Mexico's most acclaimed composers. He founded and became conductor of the Symphony Orchestra of Mexico in 1928. His music was influenced by modern American and European music, traditional Indian rhythms and Mexican folk songs.

SOR JUANA INÉS DE LA CRUZ (1651–1695) Born in San Miguel Nepantla, this colonial Mexican woman was the most famous poet of her day. She entered a convent, where she studied, played musical instruments and wrote. Her fame and independent ideas upset the archbishop of Mexico, who persecuted her. She died during an epidemic aged forty-four, but her poetry lives on.

VICENTE FOX (b 1942) Starting his career as a delivery van driver, Fox became a top executive with Coca-Cola in Mexico and finally president of the country. He is a member of the right-of-centre National Action Party (PAN). In 1995 he was elected governor of his home state of Guanajuato, where he owns a ranch. At fifty-eight he became Mexico's sixty-second president. Fox offered a grassroots approach to politics and promised change, sparking great optimism. He was born in Mexico City.

CARLOS FUENTES (b 1928) Born in Panama, but raised in Mexico, Fuentes is a prolific essayist, playwright and novelist. His father was a diplomat, so he travelled extensively as a child. In the mid-1970s, he himself served as ambassador to France. His writings explore Mexico's history, cultural identity and future challenges.

MIGUEL HIDALGO Y COSTILLO (FATHER HIDALGO) (1753–1811) A priest in the town of Dolores (now Dolores Hidalgo), he tried to improve conditions for his poor parishioners. He was part of a group that wanted Mexico to become independent of Spain. In 1810 he rang the church bells to call the parishioners together and led a rebel force of sixty thousand people. He was eventually captured, found guilty of treason and executed. Mexicans revere Father Hidalgo as father of the nation, and his call for independence is repeated every year. He was born in Pénjamo, Guanajuato.

BENITO JUÁREZ (1806–1872) A Zapotec Indian from Oaxaca state, he became president of Mexico in 1855. His parents died when he was small, and he worked in the fields until he was twelve. Then he walked to the nearby city of Oaxaca to stay with his sister so he could get an education. He attended law school, then entered politics. As president, he introduced important reforms.

FRIDA KAHLO (1907–1954) A highly regarded and talented painter born in Mexico City, she often used her own life as subject matter for her work. Her father was a German photographer, her mother a Mexican. She lived in pain most of her life after an accident in which a bus she was riding collided with a tram. She was well known for her tempestuous marriage to muralist Diego Rivera and her flamboyant style of dress and painting.

DOÑA MARINA (c1500-c1527) Born in the state of Jalisco, this young Aztec woman (also known as *La Malinche*) became Hernán Cortés's mistress. She spoke Maya, Nahuátl and Spanish and translated for the conquistadors. She also advised them, helping them to defeat the Aztecs. Some people scorn her for being a traitor to her people.

OCTAVIO PAZ (1914–1998) This poet, philosopher and writer from Mexico City won the Nobel Prize for Literature in 1990. His best-known book, *The Labyrinth of Solitude,* examines the attributes of Mexican people. He was also a diplomat, acting as Mexico's ambassador to India from 1962 to 1968. He resigned to protest the massacre of student protesters in Tlatelolco that year.

JOSÉ GUADALUPE POSADA (1852–1913) This cartoonist's engravings are still familiar. He owned a shop in Mexico City, where he printed tabloid newspapers featuring stories of crime and the bizarre. One of his best-known images portrays a skeleton wearing a fancy feathered hat. Posada was born in the state of Aguascalientes.

DIEGO RIVERA (1886–1957) Born in Guanajuato, Rivera showed talent at a very young age and received a scholarship at twenty to study art in Europe. When he came back, the government hired him to paint huge murals on the walls of many public buildings. Much of his work includes political themes, and he was inspired by Mexico's indigenous peoples and their arts. Rivera was married to painter Frida Kahlo.

FRANCISCO 'PANCHO' VILLA (1878–1923) He was a legendary and charismatic leader of the Mexican Revolution. He was born in Durango and grew up in the northern state of Chihuahua and combined his guerilla forces with those of Emiliano Zapata, from the south. With his beard, big sombrero and ammunition belt slung across his chest, Villa fit the image of the revolutionary fighter.

EMILIANO ZAPATA (1879–1919) This revolutionary leader was born to a very poor family in the state of Morelos. He learned to read and write and became a horse trader and farmer. In 1909 he was elected to his village council. When the revolution broke out a year later, he led a group of mostly Indian farmer fighters as they destroyed sugar haciendas, captured several cities and eventually fought their way to Mexico City. He formulated the rebels' demands, including land redistribution to the farmers. He was ambushed and killed in 1919.

ALAMEDA CENTRAL, MEXICO CITY This park was named after the many *álamos*, or poplar trees, planted here in the late 1500s. Next to the park is the spectacular Palacio de Bellas Artes theatre, with an interior that includes murals painted by famous Mexican artists, including Diego Rivera, José Clemente Orozco and David Siqueiros.

CHICHÉN ITZÁ This is the best-preserved Maya archaeological site on the Yucatán Peninsula. Archaeologists are not certain when the buildings were constructed, but the site includes an astronomical observatory, a pyramid dedicated to the Maya god Kukulcán, a large ball court and several other structures.

COZUMEL ISLAND Located off the east coast of the Yucatán Peninsula, Cozumel is Mexico's largest island and a popular tourist destination. People come to dive in the coral reefs off the island's sheltered beaches. The reef has a rich variety of marine life.

CUERNAVACA In this colonial city south of Mexico City is the Palacio de Cortés. Hernán Cortés built this fortress from the ruins of the Aztec pyramids he destroyed. He lived in the palace with his Spanish wife for ten years until he returned to Spain in 1540. The building is adorned with murals by Diego Rivera and is home to a regional museum.

MONTE ALBÁN This is the spectacular mountaintop ruin of what was once a ceremonial site in a great Zapotec city overlooking the Oaxaca valley. The site was first used by the Olmecs in about 500 BC. Between AD 200 and 900, the Zapotecs made Monte Albán an important economic, cultural and religious centre, but they abandoned it around 900. Later, the Mixtecs used the site for elaborate burials.

OAXACA Birthplace of reformer Benito Juárez, this large industrial and commercial centre in southern Mexico retains its historic, colonial charm. Every Saturday, the Zapotec and Mixtec Indians of the area gather at the market to sell their handicrafts, such as textiles and the green and black pottery distinctive of the region.

EL ROSARIO MONARCH BUTTERFLY SANCTUARY Located in eastern Michoacán, the El Rosario Monarch Butterfly Sanctuary is one of perhaps a dozen butterfly refuges in the highlands of Michoacán and Mexico. However, only El Rosario and one other are open to the public. Every year an estimated 100 million monarch butterflies arrive in Michoacán as part of their remarkable winter migration. The sight of so many butterflies in the sanctuary is breathtaking – the tall pines and firs are turned a blazing orange. The monarchs arrive in late October or early November and depart for their summer homes in the United States of America and Canada in early March or April, so El Rosario makes a great winter holiday destination.

SAN FRANCISCO JAVIER CHURCH Built in the majestic baroque style in the late 1600s, this church was given a new churrigueresque facade and tower in the 1700s. The church is part of the Museo Nacional del Virreinato, just north of Mexico City, which features colonial art and artefacts.

TAXCO This colonial mining town, south west of Mexico City, is over 1,800 m above sea level. Silver deposits were first discovered in Taxco in 1534. Visitors come from all over the world to look for jewellery and other silver items in the city's three hundred shops.

VIZCAÍNO BIOSPHERE RESERVE This 25,000-sq-km (9,600-square-mile) nature reserve encompasses stretches of both the east and west coasts of Baja California. It includes several islands, whale sanctuaries, a volcano, sand dunes, coastal mangroves and dry highland plateaus. Animals found in the reserve include bighorn sheep, elephant seals, ospreys and sea turtles.

ZÓCALO, MEXICO CITY The proper name of the capital's main square is Plaza de la Constitución, but most people just refer to it as the Zócalo. This is the historic heart of the city, surrounded by the Supreme Court building, the Palacio Nacional, and the imposing Catedral Metropolitana, a building that housed the first printing press in North America (dating from 1536). In one corner of the square are the excavated remains of an Aztec temple.

creoles: people of European descent who were born in colonial Mexico

deciduous forest: a forest consisting mainly of broad-leaved trees that shed all their leaves during one season. Deciduous forests are found in middle-latitude regions, like the United Kingdom.

deforestation: the clearing of forests

ecosystem: a community of organisms, such as insects and animals, and their environment that together make up an ecological unit

ejido: a communal or village landholding shared by indigenous farmers of Mexico. Most plots are too small to be farmed efficiently, and many ejidos are on poor-quality land that can't even produce enough maize and beans for the farmers' families. Some ejidos are run cooperatively by a group of people and are more financially successful.

frescoes: paintings made with water-based pigments on freshly spread plaster on walls or ceilings.

globalization: a trend toward connecting cultures through telecommunications technologies and interdependent economies, leading to a faster flow of information and commerce from country to country

hacienda: a large country estate in colonial Mexico

indigenous: native or original to an area

maquiladora: a Mexican manufacturing plant in duty-free zones along the US border

mestizos: Mexicans with mixed European and indigenous ancestry

monopoly: exclusive control in a particular market

NAFTA: The North American Free Trade Agreement, a pact that was signed by Canadian prime minister Brian Mulroney, Mexican president Carlos Salinas de Gortari and US president George Bush in 1992 and went into effect on 1 January, 1994. NAFTA provided for the gradual reduction of tariffs, customs duties and other trade barriers among the three countries and gave US and Canadian companies greater access to Mexican markets in banking, insurance, advertizing, telecommunications and road haulage .

peninsulares: European-born people who emigrated to colonial Mexico

peso: the unit of Mexican currency

soil erosion: the slow destruction or disappearance of soil, which often occurs when land that has been farmed blows away in the wind or is washed downhill by rainfall. Soil erosion is a major problem in the tropics, where high rainfall and steeply sloping ground contribute to the loss of soil that has been exposed by agriculture.

tectonic: relating to the structure of the earth's crust

viceroy: the governor of a colony

Dworkin, Mark J *Mayas, Aztecs and Incas: Mysteries of Ancient Civilizations of Central and South America.* Toronto: McClelland & Stewart, 1990.
This book is a good introduction to these fascinating ancient civilizations.

Europa Publications. *Europa World Yearbook, 2000.* London: Europa Publications, 2000.
This annual guide to countries of the world describes recent political events and lists many useful statistics and contacts.

Fuentes, Carlos. *A New Time for Mexico.* New York: Farrar, Straus & Giroux, 1996.
This is an analysis of contemporary Mexico, with insights into the revolution, democracy and Mexico's indigenous heritage, by one of Mexico's best-known authors.

Gale Research. *Statistical Abstract of the World, 1994.* Detroit: Gale Research, 1994.
This reference book has economic, social and government data from around the world.

Hellman, Judith Adler. *Mexican Lives.* New York: The New Press, 1999.
This book describes the daily lives and thoughts of a variety of Mexican individuals, rich and poor, urban and rural.

INEGI. N.d.
Website: <http://www.inegi.gob.mx/difusion/ingles/portadai.html> (n.d.)
The English-language homepage of the Instituto Nacional de Estadistica, Geografia e Informatica is a useful source of statistics from the Mexican government.

Library of Congress, Federal Research Division.
Website: <http://lcweb2.loc.gov/frd/cs/mxtoc.html> (n.d.)
The section of this excellent online resource called 'Mexico – A Country Study' includes a survey of Mexican history, as well as contemporary descriptions of the country's economy and social services.

Mader, Ron. *Mexico: Adventures in Nature.* Santa Fe: John Muir Publications, 1998.
This travel book focuses on the plants and animals of Mexico and the best places to see them.

Mexico. Eyewitness Travel Guides. New York: DK Publishing, 1999.
This travel guide is a rich source of details about every corner of Mexico and is well illustrated with photographs and maps.

Mexico Channel. N.d.
Website: <http://www.mexicochannel.net> (n.d.)
This is one of the most comprehensive websites for links to news, business, sports, music, holidays and government. You can use it in English or Spanish .

Mexico Connect. N.d.
Website: <http://www.mexconnect.com> (n.d.)
This English-language online magazine has a variety of feature articles about life in Mexico.

Selected Bibliography

Miller, Robert Ryal. *Mexico: A History.* **Norman, OK: University of Oklahoma Press, 1985.**
This book provides a thorough but easy-to-read introduction to Mexican history.

Population Reference Bureau. **N.d.**
Website: <http://www.prb.org> (n.d.)
You can search this reliable resource for world population statistics such as birth rates, population growth forecasts, HIV incidence and others.

Riding, Alan. *Distant Neighbors: A Portrait of the Mexicans.* **New York: Vintage Books, 2000.**
This insightful book, originally written in 1984 by a journalist who spent many years in Mexico, has been updated with a new foreword.

Simon, Joel. *Endangered Mexico: An Environment on the Edge.* **San Francisco: Sierra Club Books, 1997.**
This book provides an account of the many environmental problems facing Mexico.

Turner, Barry, ed. *The Statesman's Yearbook: The Politics, Cultures and Economics of the World, 2001.* **New York: Macmillan Press, 2000.**
This book has succinct statistical information and facts about the countries of the world, including Mexico.

Baquedano, Elizabeth. *Aztec, Inca, & Maya* (DK Eyewitness Books), Dorling Kindersley Publishing, 2005.
This picture-packed book takes readers back in time to when these three incredible civilizations ruled Mexico.

BBC Country Profiles – Mexico
Website: <http://news.bbc.co.uk/2/hi/americas/country_profiles>
This site has a lot of up-to-date information and statistics, as well as a timeline. You can also listen to Mexico's national anthem.

Bingham, Jane. *The Aztec Empire* (Time Travel Guides) Raintree, 2007.
This books contains information on classical civilizations and the archaeological work carried out to reveal how our ancestors lived long ago.

Lewis, Elizabeth. *Mexican Art and Culture* (World Art and Culture) Raintree Publishers, 2004.
This book explores the fine arts, the decorative arts and design through the ages of Mexican culture.

McCulloch, Julie. *Mexico* (World of Recipes) Heinemann, 2001.

Parker, Ed. *Mexico City* (Global Cities) Evans Brothers Ltd, 2006.
This book reveals reasons for the city's location and the structure of the population and explores environmental issues such as transport, waste, pollution and wildlife, city economy, culture, leisure and tourism.

Parker, Edward. *Mexico* (Countries of the World) Evans Brothers Ltd, 2005.
An exploration of Mexico, this book examines the country's important industries, physical geography, environment and social geography.

Tidmarsh, Celia. *Mexico* (World in Focus) Hodder Wayland, 2006.
A comprehensive insight into the social and economic structure of Mexico. This book also looks back on Mexico's dramatic past.

vgsbooks.com
Website: <http://www.vgsbooks.com>
Visit vgsbooks.com, the home page of the Visual Geography Series®. You can get linked to all sorts of useful online information, including geographical, historical, demographic, cultural and economic websites. The vgsbooks.com site is a great resource for the latest news and statistics.

The Virtual Diego Rivera Web Museum
Website: <http://www.diegorivera.com/>
Here you can view many of the artist's famous murals and paintings and read a chronology of his life.

Index

Acapulco 18
agriculture 5, 18, 20, 30, 34, 37,
    61–62, 65, 66
Alamo, Battle of the 29, 66
art 50–51, 70, 71, 72
Augustín I, Emperor. *See* Iturbide,
    Augustín de
Aztec civilization 5, 16, 23–24, 40,
    42, 50, 52, 55, 66, 71, 72

béisbol (baseball) 57
bullfighting 57

Calles, Plutarcho Elías 33–34
Chávez Carlos, 70
cities 4, 5, 16–18, 31, 33, 43, 44, 46,
    47, 60
Ciudad Juárez 44
corruption 6, 36
Cortés, Hernán 16, 24, 52, 66, 71, 72
Cuernavaca 72
currency 35, 36, 55, 68

dance 42, 53–54
Díaz, Porfirio 7, 31, 67
Diego, Juan 50 66
drug abuse 7, 44, 64. *See also* health
drug smuggling 6

earthquakes 11, 65, 67
economy 5, 7, 35–36, 37, 38, 44,
    58–59, 61, 62, 67; challenges,
    63–65; Mexican Miracle, 35
education 26, 31, 35, 36, 38, 41,
    46–47, 63, 65
ejidos 30, 61
environment 7, 17, 18, 19, 45, 65

Fernández de Lizardi, José Joaquín
    52, 66
flag 54, 69
flora and fauna 4, 13–14, 19, 68, 72,
    73
food 55–57
Fox, Vicente 7, 38–39, 64, 65, 67, 70
Fuentes, Carlos 52, 70
fútbol (soccer) 57

government 39. *See also* politics
Guadalajara 5, 12, 17, 57, 60, 62, 68

Guanajuato (city), 18, 27, 28

haciendas 26, 27, 32, 33, 71
health 35, 41, 42, 44–46. *See also*
    drug abuse; HIV/AIDS
Hidalgo y Costilla, Miguel 27, 50,
    54, 66, 70
history: arrival of Spaniards 18, 22,
    24, 26, 55, 57, 66; Aztec
    civilization 5, 16, 23–24, 40, 42,
    50, 52, 55, 66, 71, 72; Cortés
    expedition 24–25, 52; democratic
    reform 36–37; first inhabitants 5,
    66; independence 7, 16, 28–31, 50,
    66; Mayan civilization 5, 14,
    21–23, 42, 49, 50, 52, 55, 66, 72;
    Mexican-American War 7, 30, 66,
    67; Mexican Revolution, 7, 32–33,
    51, 67, 71; modern era 34–39;
    Porfiriato dictatorship 7, 31–32,
    67; rebellion in Chiapas 7, 37–38;
    Spanish colonial period 7, 16, 17,
    25–27, 50, 51, 56, 66, 70
HIV/AIDS 45–46
holidays: Christmas 54, 55; Cinco de
    Mayo 54; Constitution Day 54;
    Day of the Dead 55; Feast of the
    Virgin of Guadalupe 49;
    Independence Day 54; New Year's
    Day 54; *posada* 55
Huichol Indians 48

industry 4, 7, 17, 18, 19, 31, 34, 35,
    60–61, 65, 67
Iturbide, Augustín de (Emperor
    Augustín I) 28

Juárez, Benito 30–31, 54, 67, 70

Kahlo, Frida 70, 71

language 4, 11, 40, 41, 42, 48–49, 52,
    68, 71
literature 52, 66

maps 6, 15
Mayan civilization 5, 14, 21–23, 42,
    49, 50, 52, 55, 66, 72
media 52–53, 65
Mexico: boundaries, location and

size 4, 8, 11, 68; currency 35, 36, 55, 68; flag 54, 69; flora and fauna 4, 13–14, 19, 68, 72, 73; government 39; maps 6, 15; national anthem 69; politics 7, 29, 33, 38, 70; population 4, 5, 14, 16, 17, 18, 32, 35, 38, 40–41, 42, 43–44, 45, 49, 63

Mexico City 5, 8, 11, 16–17, 22, 25, 26, 30, 31, 35, 38, 39, 44, 46, 50, 52, 57, 60, 61, 62, 66, 67, 68, 71, 72, 73

Mixtec Indians 22, 42, 66, 72

Moctezuma II 24–25, 66

Monterrey 5, 18, 60, 62, 68

music 17, 27, 53, 54, 55, 70

national anthem 69

natural resources 5, 18, 26, 31, 35, 60–61, 67, 73

North American Free Trade Agreement (NAFTA) 36, 37, 58, 64, 67, 74

Olmec civilization 21, 22, 66, 72

Orozco, José Clemente 51, 72

Paz, Octavio 52, 67, 71

peso. *See* currency

Petróleos Mexicanos (PEMEX) 34, 60

politics 7, 29, 33, 38, 70; Democratic Revolution Party 38; Institutional Revolutionary Party (PRI) 7, 33, 36, 37, 38, 67; National Action Party (PAN) 38. *See also* government

pollution 6, 17, 19, 65

population 4, 5, 14, 16, 17, 18, 32, 35, 38, 40–41, 42, 43–44, 45, 49, 63

poverty 6, 17, 35, 38, 39, 65

Puebla (city) 5, 11, 18, 20, 31, 54, 56, 67, 68

recipe 56

regions 5, 7, 11, 12, 14, 18, 19, 20, 21, 24, 25, 27, 28, 29, 35, 41, 43, 44, 48, 55, 56, 60, 61, 62, 64, 65, 71; Baja California Peninsula 10, 11, 12, 18, 68, 73; Chiapas Highlands 10, 13, 21, 68; Gulf Coastal Plain 10, 68; Mesa del Norte 9; Mexican Plateau 8–9, 11, 12, 22, 68; Pacific Coastal Lowlands 10, 12, 13, 68; Valley of Mexico 9, 23; Yucatán Peninsula 8, 10, 13, 14, 18, 21, 22, 42, 48, 61, 72

religion 26, 30, 37, 40, 41, 42, 48, 49–50, 54, 55

Rivera, Diego 51, 67, 70, 71, 72

Salinas de Gortari, Carlos 36, 37, 67

Santa Anna, Antonio López de 29–30

Siqueiros, David Alfaro 51, 72

social classes 27, 28, 32, 37, 39, 41, 64

sports 57

states 14, 39, 44, 46; Baja California Sur 14, 43; Chiapas 7, 14, 37, 38, 48, 67; Chihuahua 12, 14, 48, 71; Distrito Federal 14, 43; Durango 14, 18; Guanajuato 14, 18, 43, 70, 71; Guerrero 14; Jalisco 14, 53; México 14, 43; Michoacán 14; Oaxaca 14, 22, 42, 56, 70, 72; Puebla 14, 18, 22, 43; Sonora 18, 19; Tabasco 12, 14, 18; Tlaxcala 14; Veracruz 12, 14, 18; Zacatecas 14

Tarahumara Indians 48, 72

Taxco 73

Tijuana 44

Tlaxcalan Indians 24, 25

Toltec civilization 22, 23, 66

trade 7, 39, 58–59

United States 4, 7, 8, 9, 10, 11, 19, 36, 43, 44, 45, 48, 53, 55, 57, 58, 60, 61, 63, 64, 65, 66; relationship with Mexico 63–64

Veracruz (city) 18, 21, 24, 31, 62, 66

Villa, Francisco 'Pancho' 33, 71

volcanoes 4, 9; Ixtaccihuatl, 9; Orizaba (Citlaltépetl) 9; Popocatépetl 9, 11

Zapata, Emiliano 33, 37, 67, 71

Zapatista National Liberation Army 37, 38

Zapotec Indians 22, 30, 42, 66, 70, 72

Captions for photos appearing on cover and chapter openers:

Cover: The Mayan ruins at Chichén Itzá are renowned for their stark beauty.

pp 4–5 Chillies, a staple of Mexican cooking, hang in bunches to dry in the sun.

pp 8–9 The majestic though almost inaccessible Copper Canyon in the state of Chihuahua is Mexico's 'Grand Canyon'.

pp 20–21 The awe-inspiring ruins of the ancient city of Monte Albán, which served as the hub of activity for the Zapotec people for nearly seven hundred years.

pp 40–41 Schoolchildren pose for a photographer.

pp 48–49 Mariachi singers perform at a mariachi festival.

pp 58–59 This photograph shows Mexican bills in denominations of 20 and 50 pesos.

Photo Acknowledgements

The images in this book are used with the permission of: © D. Cavagnaro/Visuals Unlimited, pp. 4-5; © PresentationMaps.com, pp. 7, 15; © Buddy Mays/TRAVEL STOCK, pp. 8-9, 13, 62; © Suzanne Murphy-Larronde, pp. 10, 14, 40-41, 44, 45, 48-49, 50, 53; © Danny Lehman/CORBIS, p. 12; © Randy Faris/CORBIS, pp. 16-17; © A.A.M. Van der Heyden/Independent Picture Service, pp. 20-21, 23; Library of Congress, pp. 24, 32 (LC-USZ62-25481), 33 (LC-DIG-npcc-12547); © Schalkwijk/Art Resource, NY, pp. 28, 51; © Bettmann/CORBIS, p. 29; Collection of The New-York Historical Society, negative #6409, accession #1878.3, p. 30; © Sergio Dorantes/CORBIS, pp. 34, 43; AP Photo/Damian Dovarganes, p. 36; © Reuters/CORBIS, pp. 37, 39, 65; © Charles & Josette Lenars/CORBIS, p. 42; © Baynard H. Brattstrom/Visuals Unlimited, p. 46; © Stephanie Maze/CORBIS, pp. 46-47; © Vittoriano Rastelli/CORBIS, p. 52; © Independent Picture Service, p. 54; © Robert Fried/robertfriedphotography.com, p. 56; © W. Lynn Seldon, Jr., p. 57; © Todd Strand/Independent Picture Service, pp. 58-59, 68; © Tenneco, Inc./Independent Picture Service, p. 60; © Steve McCutcheon/Visuals Unlimited, p. 61; © Laura Westlund/Independent Picture Service, p. 69.

Front Cover: © A.A.M. Van der Heyden/Independent Picture Service

Back Cover: NASA